The CD-ROM included with *YOUR ROOTS* contains a variety of forms, shareware programs, and software demos, all designed to help you take advantage of the many genealogy resources available to you by computer as you plan your genealogy exploration. In addition, you'll get $15 worth of free time on CompuServe, the popular online service.

Here are the demos you'll find on the CD-ROM:

- Family Origins for Windows and Family Origins for DOS
- The Master Genealogist
- Reunion for Windows
- Family Tree Maker for Windows
- Roots IV for DOS

In addition to these demos, you find the shareware program Brother's Keeper and Family Tree for Windows. And the CD-ROM also contains these forms and information:

- Census Inquiry Forms
- Family Information Form
- Genealogy Dictionary (glossary of buzzwords)
- Factfinder for the Nation (listing available census records)
- Directory of National Archives
- Addresses of all Vital Records offices in the United States
- Card file (alphabetical listing of over 5,000 genealogy societies, libraries, and archives throughout North America)
- National Genealogy Society membership and resource information
- New England Historic Genealogical Society

You'll also discover the exciting world of CompuServe, where you can share information with people around the world. Included on this CD-ROM is WinCIM for Windows, a colorful, easy-to-use interface program, and $15 of online time through ZiffNet.

System Requirements

- 386DX-33 (486DX-33 or faster recommended)
- 4MB RAM (minimum)
- 4MB available on hard drive
- SuperVGA adapter (supporting 640 × 480 resolution and 256 colors) highly recommended
- Microsoft Mouse or 100 percent compatible
- Microsoft Windows 3.1 or higher
- MS-DOS 3.0 or higher
- Single-speed CD-ROM drive (double-speed recommended)

PLEASE NOTE—USE OF THE CD-ROM AND THE PROGRAMS INCLUDED ON THE CD-ROM PACKAGED WITH THIS BOOK AND THE PROGRAM LISTINGS INCLUDED IN THIS BOOK IS SUBJECT TO AN END-USER LICENSE AGREEMENT (THE "AGREEMENT") FOUND AT THE BACK OF THE BOOK. PLEASE READ THE AGREEMENT CAREFULLY BEFORE MAKING YOUR PURCHASE DECISION. PURCHASE OF THE BOOK AND USE OF THE CD-ROM, PROGRAMS, AND PROGRAM LISTINGS WILL CONSTITUTE ACCEPTANCE OF THE AGREEMENT.

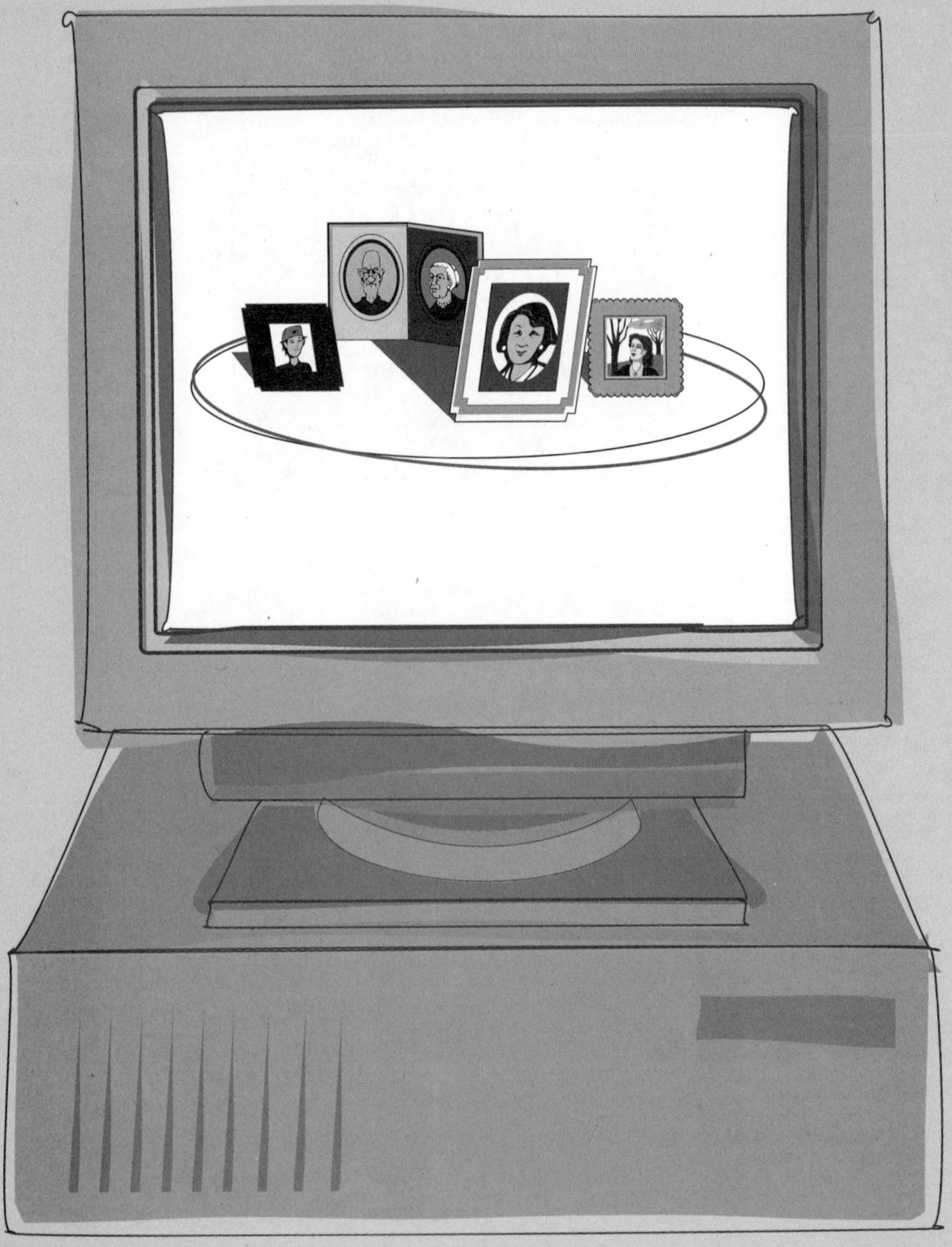

YOUR ROOTS:
Total *Genealogy* *Planning* on *Your* *Computer*

Richard Eastman

ZIFF-DAVIS PRESS
EMERYVILLE, CALIFORNIA

Editor	Margo Hill
Project Coordinator	Barbara Dahl
Proofreader	Vanessa Miller
Cover Design and Illustration	Regan Honda
Book Design	Regan Honda
Screen Graphics Editor	P. Diamond
Illustration	Cherie Plumlee, Sarah Ishida, and Mina Reimer
Word Processing	Howard Blechman
Page Layout	Alan Morgenegg and Tony Jonick
Indexer	Valerie Robbins

Ziff-Davis Press books are produced on a Macintosh computer system with the following applications: FrameMaker®, Microsoft® Word, QuarkXPress®, Adobe Illustrator®, Adobe Photoshop®, Adobe Streamline™, MacLink®*Plus*, Aldus® FreeHand™, Collage Plus™.

For information about U.S. rights and permissions, contact Chantal Tucker at Ziff-Davis Publishing, fax 212-503-5420.

If you have comments or questions or would like to receive a free catalog, call or write:
Ziff-Davis Press
5903 Christie Avenue
Emeryville, CA 94608
800-688-0448

ISBN 1-56276-326-1

Manufactured in the United States of America
10 9 8 7 6 5 4 3 2 1

This

book is dedicated in loving memory of my son Christopher. While it is interesting to study ancestry, we may only take pride in our descendants. We all miss you, Chris.

Table of Contents

The study of genealogy is almost as old as humanity. It is mentioned in the Bible and in other ancient books. In ancient times, the few people who were literate used a brush and parchment to record such information. In later years, the technology changed to quill pens and paper, then to ballpoint pens and index cards. Each of these steps reduced the work involved and made genealogy available to more people, but modern computers, databases, and other technology tools have made it easier to trace one's family tree than ever before.

Today you can sit at home and compare notes online with other people who have similar interests. You can use a specialized genealogy program to record information about your ancestors and include scanned photographs. You can search databases on CD-ROMs—a resource that was not available to genealogists just a few years ago. You may need to leave the comfort of your living room to search microfilm at a nearby facility, but that is inexpensive and easy to do. All of these activities are described in this book in detail.

For most people genealogy is a hobby; it is done simply for curiosity. But with a proper genealogy program you can record the names, dates, places, and biographical details of your ancestors, and chart the inherited medical conditions you were born with. You can probably determine where you obtained the color of your eyes, the color of your hair, and the gap between your front teeth, as well as your tendency for high blood pressure, or other medical information that you and your doctor are interested in. By studying your ancestry you may possibly prolong your own life and well-being, along with that of your relatives.

As you progress in your genealogy searches you will probably find a few black sheep in the family tree along with a few notables of some sort. In other words, your family tree is much like everyone else's. You should cherish the black sheep as much as you do the others: They are the ones who often make all this research interesting.

This book will show you the techniques and tools required to start your genealogy search. To find your ancestors you do not need a powerful computer. (After all, people have been doing genealogy work for centuries without one.) The PC or Macintosh that you presently own will probably work fine. You may want to add a scanner, modem, CD-ROM drive, and some other peripherals to your present system, this book will guide you in the selection of the devices you can use for genealogy work.

This book was written partly out of frustration. As the manager of the Genealogy Forum on CompuServe, I am frequently asked how to find information or how to accomplish specific tasks in genealogy research. I can usually refer to a book or to some other source on a particular topic. But I was never able to refer to any one beginner's book that covered all the topics that the genealogy newcomer should learn today. The few books that have been written as introductory genealogy texts were all written before the explosion of home computers and online systems and genealogy CD-ROMs. This book is an attempt to fill that gaping hole.

I'd love to hear from you about how you've used the ideas in this book. I can be reached on CompuServe's Genealogy Forum by GO ROOTS. Anyone who can send e-mail to an Internet address can reach me at **76701.263@compuserve.com**.

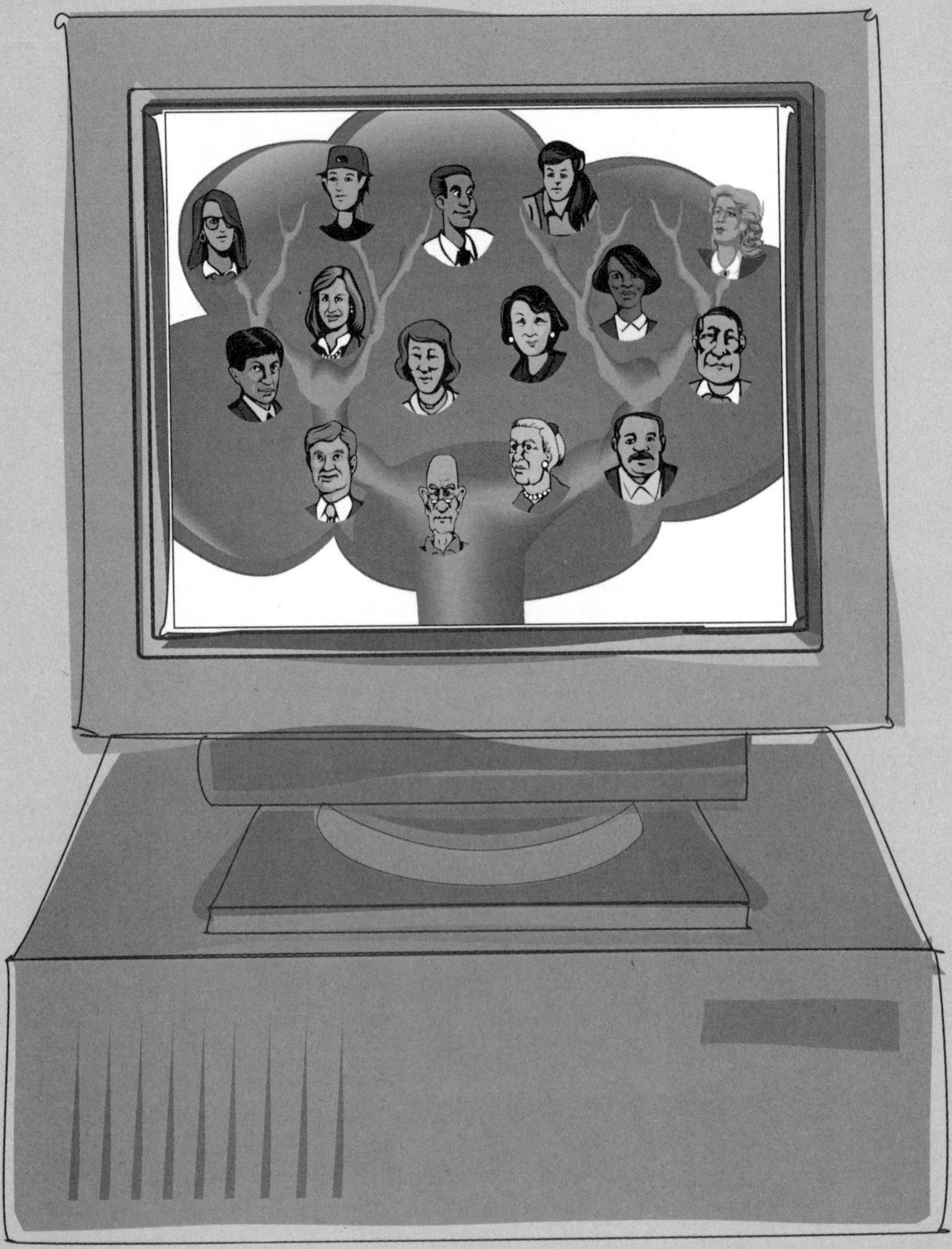

1

Welcome to the World of Computerized Genealogy

Tracing

Tracing your ancestry is interesting and exciting. Finding out who you are and where your ancestors came from is one of the most fascinating projects that you can ever accomplish.

Where did your last name originate? Your mother's maiden name? What countries can you claim as your ancestral homelands? Is there a coat of arms associated with your family name? Where did you get your hair color? That gap between your front teeth? Are you perhaps prone to high blood pressure or some other medical condition inherited from your ancestors? These are just a few of the questions that you can answer by studying your family history.

Anyone Can Do It

Whether your ancestors stepped off the Mayflower or arrived by way of Ellis Island or any of a dozen other entry points is not terribly important. There are family records available for almost all cultures, whether your heritage is from Europe, Africa, the Orient, Latin America or is American Indian. It is not necessary to trace your ancestry back hundreds of years; many people find pleasure in knowing four or five generations and in studying the conditions in which those ancestors lived. Of course, once you have the first few generations recorded, you can always go back at any time and try to push back even a few years earlier to yet another and then another generation. Not every ancestor needed to have blue blood in order to leave records. Many people have been able to trace working class ancestry back into the Middle Ages. Genealogy is a hobby that is rapidly growing as many people become interested in their family roots.

How far back can you trace? There is no definitive answer, but many people have been pleasantly surprised at how easily they have been able to trace their ancestry six or eight or even more generations. You may be able to find even earlier generations in this country or in "the old countries," wherever they may be. By combining both computer databases and other traditional research techniques, you do not have to travel to distant lands to look at records. Information is often available to you at home or at a location near you.

You may not find every single ancestor in the past 300 years, but you often can find hundreds of ancestors when researching your full family tree. Most people do trace both paternal and maternal ancestors, not simply their father's father's father's ancestors. You will want to know about as many of your ancestors as possible, including the maternal branches of the family tree.

Various public records have existed in North America since the arrival of the first European settlers. Not everyone's birth was recorded and not every public record has survived, but by far the majority of these people have left some records. Even when birth records are missing, census records, church records, military records, pension application forms, land sales, old wills, and the ever-present tax collectors' records all contain valuable information. Some of these records, most notably census records, are now beginning to appear on computer CD-ROM discs.

Western European countries generally have good records. In some villages records have been preserved from the Middle Ages listing the christenings and marriages of all the villagers as well as the lists of taxes collected for centuries. Scandinavian records are also noted for being well preserved in large quantities. Eastern Europeans have more difficulty, as do Asians. Yet it's often possible to go back 100 or more years in those countries too.

For many years Black Americans did not study their genealogies seriously, as there was a popular belief that Black ancestry was impossible to trace. Of course that belief did not stop Alex Haley, who single-handedly started a genealogy revolution with his book *Roots*.

When I began tracing my ancestry, I ignored my mother's French-Canadian heritage. I thought that it would be too difficult to find records in a foreign language and that those records would be located some distance away from where I lived. Besides, older family members had told me that these ancestors were almost all laborers and woodsmen and that there would be very few records available for them or their origins. When I finally plunged into the records from Quebec province and from Acadia (the old name for what is now Nova Scotia and a part of New Brunswick), I was delighted to find excellent records that were readily available on microfilm and in books.

I was able to trace almost all of my French-speaking ancestors' origins back to France in the early 1600s, and a few families had records well back into the Middle Ages. Also, this collection of several thousand ancestors included a wide assortment of laborers, shopkeepers, farmers, woodsmen, some nobility, and several large landowners, as well as a delightful assortment of ne'er-do-wells. In short, my family tree is about like everyone else's.

I never needed to go to Quebec or elsewhere to find the records. Instead, I have been able to find all the information I needed by visiting libraries and Family History Centers within a few miles of my home. If I were starting today it would be even easier, as some of those same records have since been computerized. Your ancestry can probably be traced regardless of the nationalities involved.

How Computers Can Help You Research

Many people think (or at least hope) that they can dial into an online database, push a few buttons, and have their entire ancestry for several centuries revealed. This may be true someday, but it's doubtful that we will see such databases online in the twentieth century.

While you cannot instantly find all your ancestors within a single database, use of a home computer can still simplify and speed your search for the family tree. There are many CD-ROM discs of genealogy information available today. You can compare notes and seek assistance from others using online systems. A modern genealogy software program will allow you to store and organize information and to retrieve that data quickly and easily whenever you want and in the format that you want. You can organize and print information quickly and easily. Many genealogy programs will even print your data in a computer-generated "book" that is easily read by non-genealogists. You can even print out customized "My Ancestry" books for other members of your family, each book starting with that person on page one and then showing their ancestry on successive pages.

There are CD-ROM databases that you can purchase or rent, or you can travel to genealogy libraries and use the CD-ROM discs there. Later in this book you will find detailed information on how to use the computerized databases available on CD-ROM discs from the Church of Jesus Christ of Latter-day Saints (the Mormons). Those databases are available to everyone, regardless of religion. The information there may be transferred to a floppy disk that you can later import to your own genealogy database.

Genealogy Online

By using a modem and a communications program you can easily compare notes with others worldwide who may share ancestry with you; they can help you and vice versa. You may need suggestions from others more familiar with records in a certain area or time frame. Again, there are people around the world who can and will help. You can contact more genealogy "experts" by use of a modem than you ever could by personal visits or by writing letters.

When I started researching my ancestry, I labored almost alone. I talked with my older relatives and a few others, but almost all the research work was done in isolation. At times I felt that I was going down the same path as many people ahead of me, but I did not have the benefit of seeing their results. I had no method of finding others who were researching in the same areas that I was except by an occasional lucky coincidence.

Today you can sit at home and dial a local telephone number with your computer. The result is that your computer is connected to a mainframe computer located perhaps thousands of miles away. You can then compare notes with other people who are researching the same family names or else researching in the same area's records. If you need to know where a certain small town is in Europe, or perhaps find out detailed information about emigration from a foreign land, you can easily exchange electronic messages with residents of those countries who also have an interest in genealogy. They can often offer an insight that you will never find in printed books, at least not in any book printed in English. You can post a message describing the information you seek, and your message will be visible to tens of thousands of other genealogists worldwide within seconds. You can obtain assistance that would be difficult or almost impossible to obtain otherwise.

One of the big breaks in taking my ancestry back into the early Middle Ages occurred when someone who lived in another country posted a short message on CompuServe. He casually mentioned some early French-Canadian families whose ancestry had been researched and published in an obscure little book that only had a few copies printed. I recognized one of those names as being in my family tree, so I dashed off to a large city library and found a copy of the book. It did list some of my ancestors in Quebec, and then described their ancestry back to the twelfth century along with an extensive list of citations of all the records searched to verify the information contained within the book.

Without the easy access to thousands of other genealogists online, I might have spent many years of frustration without ever knowing about that little book.

Genealogy programs can be downloaded online and stored on your local disk drive to be used over and over again. You can also search some of the online databases that exist today; several of them are of interest to family historians. All you need is your computer, a modem, and a telephone line.

Genealogy Programs

When I started researching my ancestry, my primary tools were a ball-point pen and a stack of 3-by-5 inch index cards. This served as my "database." Each ancestor or other relative was recorded on a card and each card was numbered and then stored in alphabetical order. Each card contained as much information about that person as I could find; it typically included parents' names and their card numbers along with children's names and their card numbers. Each card also had space for vital information such as date and place of birth, date and place of marriage, and so forth. Text notes were recorded on the back of each card. This record keeping was tedious. Transcribing data onto a chart or a printed page was so difficult that I rarely did it. For the first few years I only identified a few hundred ancestors and relatives. I found it difficult to find, record, and organize my data.

I eventually moved the information on these cards into a computer. My first such effort was done on 80-column punch cards that were then fed into a mainframe computer that was state of the art at the time. I found that I could sort and print data in a manner that was impossible before. It was now possible to quickly find all the people with the same place of birth and to even print those records out. That was very helpful when planning a visit to a library or to the town clerk's office in a particular town. I could now enter the clerk's office carrying a computer printout listing the information I was seeking.

The fast growth of computer technology has since simplified the record-keeping tasks. Genealogists can now keep huge databases of thousands or even tens of thousands of individual records in desktop computers or even in notebook-sized PCs that are many times more powerful than the mainframes of a few years ago. A wide variety of printed reports is now available by moving a mouse and clicking a few times. Whether you want a simple list of records to be checked on your next visit to a library, or you want to print an entire book of your cousin's ancestry for a Christmas gift, you can easily do so with a modern genealogy program. In fact, you really do not need to print a list prior to visiting the library. Today's technology allows you to take your entire database with you in a five-pound laptop PC or possibly even on a palmtop computer carried in a pocket or purse.

One of the best reasons for using a modern genealogy program for recording information is the large number of people you will need to record. Assuming that you record only your direct ancestors and that you go back 300 years, that's more than 8,000 people! The following chart illustrates the progression. This chart assumes that one generation is equivalent to 25 years:

Relationship to You	Number of Individuals	Number of Years
Parents	2	25
Grandparents	4	50
Great-Grandparents	8	75
ggGrandparents	16	100
gggGrandparents	32	125
ggggGrandparents	64	150
gggggGrandparents	128	175
ggggggGrandparents	256	200
gggggggGrandparents	512	225
ggggggggGrandparents	1024	250
gggggggggGrandparents	2048	275
ggggggggggGrandparents	4096	300
Total	8190	

When reading this chart, substitute the word "great" for every lower case "g." The word "gggGrandparents" means "great-great-great-Grandparents."

The above chart shows that you have about 8,190 direct ancestors born within the past 300 years. This includes 4,096 great-great-great-great-great-great-great-great-great-great-Grandparents! By the way, it is not unusual to find the same individual two or three places (or more) in your family tree. These are "multiple lines of descent" from the same person.

Finding all of these ancestors is not impossible; some people have been able to find 8,000 or more, although 1,000 to 4,000 is probably more typical. Also, many people wish to record more than just their direct ancestors. They record information about their cousins, aunts, uncles, great-aunts, great-uncles, and so on. Often, they enter data about all their ancestors' siblings into the database. Genealogy databases of 40,000 or more people are unusual—but certainly not impossible. Imagine trying to keep track of all those people without a computer!

Whatever you do in genealogy, you should ensure that when you record the information, you verify its accuracy to the best your ability and preserve it for future generations. As you discover old records and handwritten notes made by previous genealogy researchers, you will find numerous errors. Many people simply wrote down the information they were told and never verified it. This information may or may not have been correct. Errors and misinformation are common in genealogy. There are many books containing family trees in which an estimated 10 percent of the printed information is wrong. Some of the computerized databases contain similar error rates. Yet, by cross-checking and comparing printed information against so-called primary records, you can find and eliminate most errors. Use of a computer genealogy program allows you to update and correct your records whenever necessary.

Early genealogy programs only allowed for storage of text entries, such as names, places, and dates. Today's programs normally include the capability for scanned graphics so that you may have pictures within the database. When reading information about your great-grandmother on the screen, you can even have her picture displayed if you have such a family heirloom photo. If there is some dispute as to what a handwritten entry in the 1870 census really said, enter a scanned picture of the census entry into the database and link it to the census record. Leave the database record listed as "unknown" or "questionable" and then have the actual handwriting displayed. Some genealogy programs even include the capability of full motion videos and sound clips.

Computer databases are not the only tools available to genealogists. You will undoubtedly find old photographs of family members; many of these photos will be faded, stained, or damaged in some manner. You can use computer enhancement techniques to restore photographs to like-new condition. Modern scanners and desktop computers have made these tools available to the hobbyist.

What Now?

Now that you have decided to find out more about your ancestors, you will need to make a list of objectives. This list does not need to be written down—it's a short list and one that you can easily memorize. Besides, you will probably change it often. You need to think about the "tools" that you will be using. Will you use a computer? If so, will your present computer be sufficient? Chances are that it will.

You will need a genealogy program to simplify the record keeping, but which one? If you enter all your data into one program and then later decide to switch to a more advanced program, will you need to type all that data in again? If you are careful in selecting the genealogy programs, the answer will be No. If you do a bit of planning in advance you will be able to switch back and forth between different programs with a minimum of inconvenience.

Do you need a CD-ROM disk drive? Do you need a high-speed modem? How about a laser printer? While detailed answers to these questions are contained later in this book, you can easily start off with a minimum of hardware and software. In fact, a computer isn't absolutely required, but it is much easier to do genealogy on a computer than it is to do the same thing on paper.

If you already own a computer system, then it is probably sufficient to get you started. As you become experienced in family history you will perhaps find that you can utilize newer computer tools, and you may wish to obtain them. If you are contemplating the purchase of your first computer, this book will give you the information needed to select the proper computer system for your genealogy project.

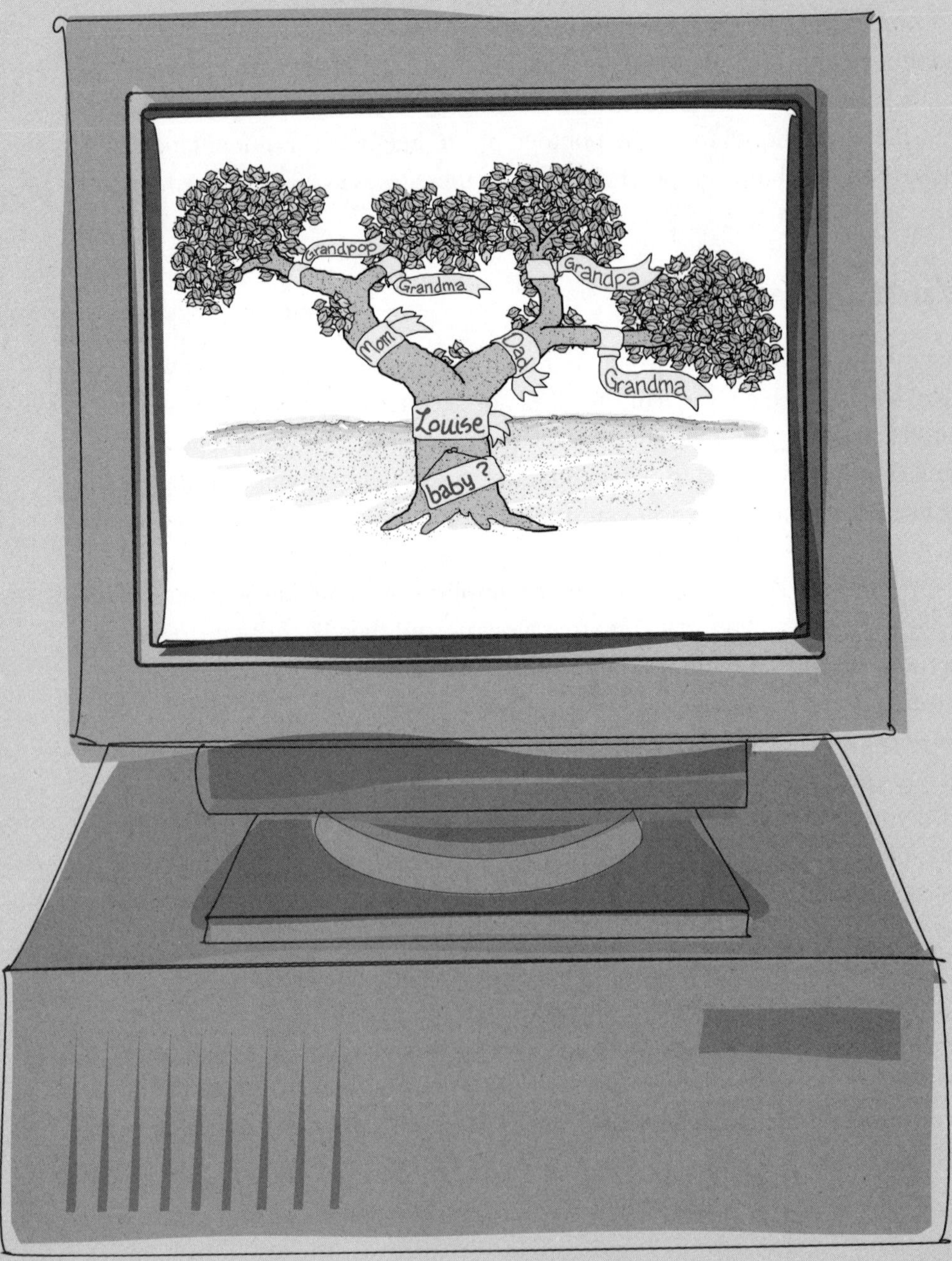
Grandpop
Grandma
Grandpa
Mom
Dad
Grandma
Louise
baby ?

2 | How to **Organize** the **Information** You Have **Gathered**

The

terminology used in genealogy may be strange to you. Genealogists use terms unique to old records and new terms associated with computer programs used for recording family information. This chapter will provide an explanation of the terms used and the record keeping methods used.

Probably the most common mistake the typical newcomer makes is in not recording all the relevant information on paper or in a computerized database. At a minimum, the names, places, and dates of each individual found need to be recorded along with a reference citation as to where the information was obtained. For instance, obtaining data from a book might be cited as "*Savage's Genealogical Dictionary of the Early Settlers of New England*, Volume 1, page 342." Likewise, a person listed in the U.S. census might be listed as "1840 U.S. Census, Town of Corinth, Penobscot County, Maine, page 15."

Recording the source of the information helps to maintain the integrity of the data when conflicting information is found. If you find something that disagrees with what you wrote down earlier, you can always go back and read the earlier record again if you know where to look. Trusting your memory is not enough—you will forget!

There are several forms for recording genealogy information on paper that are recognized as essential genealogical tools. These forms are not always identical. Different printed forms produced by different companies vary in appearance. However, they will all look somewhat similar and will be instantly recognized by the experienced genealogist. Most of the modern genealogy programs can accept data in a format similar to these forms and can always print reports in these formats. Genealogy software might be considered the modern "electronic equivalent" of paper-based record keeping.

You do not have to purchase these forms; many genealogy programs will print them for you. Also, you can obtain these forms as templates for a word processor and then print them yourself on a laser printer or high-quality inkjet printer. By printing your own forms you have the capability of customizing them in any method that you wish. Genealogy research forms for Microsoft Word and for WordPerfect may be obtained online from CompuServe's Genealogy Forum as well as from other online services.

When writing on paper forms, always use pencil so that information can be changed when necessary. Upon returning home you can transcribe the data into the computer. Always write the full maiden names for females—not their married names. Most genealogists prefer to use the day-month-year format for dates, such as: 12 Nov 1849.

Pedigree Chart

Probably the most common form used in genealogy work is the *pedigree chart*. It shows one's ancestors and gives brief information about them. Any unknown ancestors are left blank. A pedigree chart may be visualized as:

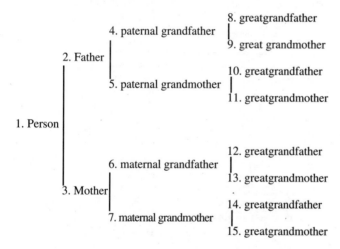

Notice the numbers shown in the above chart. The *base individual* is shown as person #1, the father is shown as #2, the mother is #3, the paternal grandfather is #4, the paternal grandmother is #5, and so on. This numbering system is referred to as *ahnentafel numbers* and will be explained at length in the section on ahnentafel reports. Not all pedigree charts use these numbers but most charts will.

The figure on the next page shows a 4-generation pedigree chart. The person to the left is the base individual with each prior generation shown to the right. In each case, to locate a person's parents find the person on the chart and then

➡ A typical pedigree chart

Pedigree Chart   Chart no. 1

No. 1 on this chart is the same as no. 1 on chart no. 1

8 Patrick KENNEDY
Born: ABT 1823   cont. ____
Place: Dunganstown, Wexford Co, Ireland
Marr: 26 Sep 1849
Place: Boston, Suffolk Co, MA
Died: 22 Nov 1858
Place: Boston, Suffolk Co, MA

4 Patrick Joseph KENNEDY
Born: 14 Jan 1858
Place: East Boston, Suffolk Co, MA
Marr: 23 Nov 1887
Place: Boston, Suffolk Co, MA
Died: 18 May 1929
Place: Boston, Suffolk Co, MA

9 Bridget MURPHY
Born: 1821   cont. ____
Place: Dunganstown, Wexford Co, Ireland
Died: 20 Dec 1888
Place: Boston, Suffolk Co, MA

2 Joseph Patrick KENNEDY
Born: 6 Sep 1888
Place: East Boston, Suffolk Co, MA
Marr: 7 Oct 1914
Place: Boston, Suffolk Co, MA
Died: 18 Nov 1969
Place: Hyannis Port, Barnstable Co, MA

10 James HICKEY
Born: 1836   cont. ____
Place: Cork, Cork Co, Ireland
Marr:
Place:
Died: 22 Nov 1900
Place: Boston, Suffolk Co, MA

5 Mary Augusta HICKEY
Born: 6 Dec 1857
Place: Winthrop, Suffolk Co, MA
Died: 20 May 1923
Place: Boston, Suffolk Co, MA

11 Margaret M. FIELD
Born: ABT 1836   cont. ____
Place:
Died: 5 Jun 1911
Place: Boston, Suffolk Co, MA

1 John Fitzgerald KENNEDY
Born: 29 May 1917
Place: Brookline, Norfolk Co, MA
Marr: 12 Sep 1953
Place: Newport, Newport Co, RI
Died: 22 Nov 1963
Place: Dallas, Dallas Co, TX

Jacqueline Lee BOUVIER
Spouse

12 Thomas FITZGERALD
Born: cont. ____
Place:
Marr: 15 Nov 1857
Place:
Died: 19 May 1885
Place: Boston, Suffolk Co, MA

6 John Francis FITZGERALD
Born: 11 Feb 1863
Place: Boston, Suffolk Co, MA
Marr: 18 Sep 1889
Place: Concord, Middlesex Co, MA
Died: 3 Oct 1950
Place: Boston, Suffolk Co, MA

13 Rosanna COX
Born: ABT 1836   cont. ____
Place:
Died: 12 Mar 1879
Place: Boston, Suffolk Co, MA

3 Rose Elizabeth FITZGERALD
Born: 22 Jul 1890
Place: Boston, Suffolk Co, MA
Died: 22 Jan 1995
Place: Hyannisport, MA

14 Michael HANNON
Born: 30 Sep 1832   cont. ____
Place:
Marr: 12 Feb 1854
Place:
Died: 1 Feb 1900
Place: Acton, Middlesex Co, MA

7 Mary Josephine HANNON
Born: 31 Oct 1865
Place: Acton, Middlesex Co, MA
Died: 8 Aug 1964
Place: Dorchester, Suffolk Co, MA

15 Mary Ann FITZGERALD
Born: ABT 1832   cont. ____
Place:
Died:
Place:

Prepared 4 Jun 1995 by:

go to the right. At the intersection of the lines, go up for the father or down for the mother. Pedigree charts normally record the dates and places of birth, marriage, and death whenever known, but no other vital information.

The 4-generation pedigree chart is limited to showing only 15 individuals, while a 5-generation chart will show 31 individuals. On a 6-generation pedigree chart there is room for 63 people although there may not be enough space for the full dates and places of birth, marriage, and death. When more generations are to be displayed, additional pages may be added. On the second page a new pedigree chart is displayed with that person shown as the base individual and his ancestors are shown to the right. This new base individual is shown along with the words "Person #1 on this page is the same as person #8 on Page 1" or something similar.

Ideally, the base individual on Page 2 should keep the same number as he had on Page 1 and his ancestors' numbers are adjusted accordingly. However, not all genealogy software programs are capable of carrying ahnentafel (see below) numbers from one page to the next. All genealogy programs available today can print pedigree charts, many of them can print five or six generations on one page.

Many genealogy programs display data on-screen in pedigree format and allow you to move around the database by moving a mouse pointer and clicking on an individual shown in a pedigree chart.

Ahnentafel

The word *ahnentafel* is derived from the German words *ahnen,* meaning ancestor, and *tafel,* meaning a list or a table. It is simply a list of one's ancestors. An ahnentafel may be thought of as a descriptive pedigree chart that is collapsed together without the drawn lines. The result is a compact listing with the ability to list many more ancestors per page than what is normally shown on a pedigree chart. The information contained within an ahnentafel is identical to that within a pedigree: names, along with places and dates of birth, marriage, and death. For instance, examine the following ahnentafel:

1 John Fitzgerald Kennedy, b. 29 May 1917 in Brookline, Norfolk Co, MA, d. 22 Nov 1963 in Dallas, Dallas Co, TX, ma. 12 Sep 1953 in Newport, Newport_Co,_RI.

2 Joseph Patrick Kennedy, b. 6 Sep 1888 in East Boston, Suffolk Co, MA, d. 18 Nov 1969 in Hyannis Port, Barnstable Co, MA, ma. 7 Oct 1914 in Boston, Suffolk Co, MA.

3 Rose Elizabeth Fitzgerald, b. 22 Jul 1890 in Boston, Suffolk Co, MA, d. 22_Jan_1995_in_Hyannisport,_MA.

4 Patrick Joseph Kennedy, b. 14 Jan 1858 in East Boston, Suffolk Co, MA, d. 18 May 1929 in Boston, Suffolk Co, MA, ma. 23 Nov 1887 in Boston, Suffolk Co, MA.

5 Mary Augusta Hickey, b. 6 Dec 1857 in Winthrop, Suffolk Co, MA, d. 20 May 1923 in Boston, Suffolk Co, MA.

6 John Francis 'Honey Fitz' Fitzgerald, b. 11 Feb 1863 in Boston, Suffolk Co, MA, d. 3 Oct 1950 in Boston, Suffolk Co, MA, ma. 18 Sep 1889 in Concord, Middlesex Co, MA.

7 Mary Josephine Hannon, b. 31 Oct 1865 in Acton, Middlesex Co, MA, d. 8 Aug_1964_in_Dorchester,_Suffolk_Co,_MA.

8 Patrick Kennedy, b. circa 1823 in Dunganstown, Wexford Co, Ireland, d. 22 Nov 1858 in Boston, Suffolk Co, MA, ma. 26 Sep 1849 in Boston, Suffolk Co, MA.

9 Bridget Murphy, b. 1821 in Dunganstown, Wexford Co, Ireland, d. 20 Dec 1888 in Boston, Suffolk Co, MA.

10 James Hickey, b. 1836 in Cork, Cork Co, Munster Province, Ireland, d. 22 Nov 1900 in Boston, Suffolk Co, MA.

11 Margaret M. Field, b. circa 1836, d. 5 Jun 1911 in Boston, Suffolk Co, MA.

12 Thomas Fitzgerald, d. 19 May 1885 in Boston, Suffolk Co, MA, ma. 15 Nov 1857.

13 Rosanna Cox, b. circa 1836, d. 12 Mar 1879 in Boston, Suffolk Co, MA.

14 Michael Hannon, b. 30 Sep 1832, d. 1 Feb 1900 in Acton, Middlesex Co, MA, ma. 12 Feb 1854.

15_Mary_Ann_Fitzgerald,_b._circa_1832.

16 Patrick Kennedy, b. in Ireland, d. in Ireland, ma. in Ireland.

17 Mary Johanna (-----), b. in Ireland, d. in Ireland.

18 Richard Murphy.

19 Mary (-----).

20 Michael Hickey.

21 Catherine Hassett.

22 Patrick Field.

23 Mary Sheehy.

24 Michael Fitzgerald.

25 Ellen Wilmouth, b. 1797, d. 16 Nov 1875 in Boston, Suffolk Co, MA.
26 Philip Cox.
27 Mary (-----).
28 John Hannon.
29 Ellen Noonan, b. 1793, d. 28 Nov 1877 in Acton, Middlesex Co, MA.
30 Edmond (Edward) Fitzgerald, b. 1798 in Ireland, d. 1883.
_____31_Mary_Linnehan._____
48 James Fitzgerald.
50 Thomas Wilmouth.
51 Bridget (-----).
_____60_*James_Fitzgerald._____

The numbers, the names, and the vital information presented in an ahnentafel are the same as those displayed in a pedigree report. Notice the numbers used in the above ahnentafel. Compare them to the simplified pedigree chart that we discussed previously:

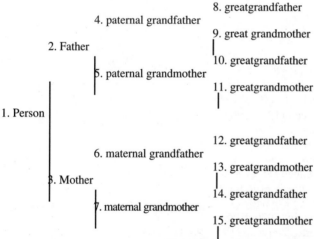

The numbers used in the pedigree chart are identical to those used in the ahnentafel. The base individual is listed as #1 with the father as #2 and the mother as #3. The grandparents are listed as numbers 4 through 7 with the paternal grandfather as #4, the paternal grandmother as #5, and so on.

You will notice that every person listed has a number and that there is a mathematical relationship among parents and children. The number of a father is always double that of the child's. The number of the mother is always double that of the child's plus one. The number of a child is always one-half that of a parent (ignoring any remainder).

In the above example, the father of person #6 is #12 (the father is double the child's number). The mother of #6 is #13 (the mother is double plus one of the child's). The child of #15 is #7. (The child is always one-half the parent's number, ignoring remainders.) These numbers work in the same manner in an ahnentafel as they do in a pedigree chart. The ahnentafel can be as long as required to list all the generations found.

Descendant Charts

Descendant charts come in all sorts of variations. They simply are a listing of one's descendants. They normally include spouses. Here is an example of one descendant chart:

```
0  1  2  3
Joseph Patrick Kennedy (1888-1969)
+Rose Elizabeth Fitzgerald (1890-1995)
 :  Joseph Patrick Kennedy Jr. (1915-1944)
 :  John Fitzgerald Kennedy (1917-1963)
 :  +Jacqueline Lee Bouvier (1929-1994)
 :  .  Caroline Bouvier Kennedy (1957- )
 :  .  +Edwin Schlossberg
 :  .  John Fitzgerald Kennedy Jr. (1960- )
 :  .  Patrick Bouvier Kennedy (1963-1963)
 :  Rosemary (Rose Marie) Kennedy (1920- )
 :  Kathleen 'Kick' Kennedy (1920-1948)
 :  +William John Robert Cavendish (1917-1944)
 :  Eunice Mary Kennedy (1921- )
 :  +Robert Sargent Shriver Jr. (1915- )
 :  .  Robert Sargent Shriver III (1954- )
 :  .  Maria Owings Shriver (1955- )
 :  .  +Arnold Shwarzenegger
 :  .  Timothy Perry Shriver (1959- )
 :  .  Mark Kennedy Shriver (1964- )
 :  .  Anthony Paul Shriver (1965- )
 :  Patricia Kennedy (1924- )
 :  +Peter Lawford (1923-1984)
 :  .  Christopher Kennedy Lawford (1955- )
```

```
:  .  +Jean Edith Olsson (1955- )
:  .  Sydney Maleia Lawford (1956- )
:  .  +James Peter McKelvey (1955- )
:  .  Victoria Francis Lawford (1958- )
:  .  Robin Elizabeth Lawford (1961- )
:  Robert Francis Kennedy (1925-1968)
:  +Ethel Skakel (1928- )
:  .  Kathleen Hartington Kennedy (1951- )
:  .  +David Lee Townsend (1947- )
:  .  .  Meaghan Anne Kennedy Townsend (1977- )
:  .  .  Maeve Fahey Kennedy Townsend (1979- )
:  .  .  Rose Katherine Kennedy Townsend (1983- )
:  .  Joseph Patrick Kennedy II (1952- )
:  .  +Sheila Brewster Rauch (1949- )
:  .  .  Joseph Patrick Kennedy III (1980- )
:  .  .  Matthew Rauch Kennedy (1980- )
:  .  Robert Francis Kennedy Jr. (1954- )
:  .  +Emily Ruth Black (1957- )
:  .  .  Robert Francis Kennedy III (1984- )
:  .  David Anthony Kennedy (1955-1984)
:  .  Mary Courtney Kennedy (1956- )
:  .  +Jeffrey Robert Ruhe (1952- )
:  .  Michael LeMoyne Kennedy (1958- )
:  .  +Victoria Denise Gifford (1957- )
:  .  .  Michael LeMoyne Kennedy Jr. (1983- )
:  .  .  Kyle Frances Kennedy (1984- )
:  .  Mary Kerry Kennedy (1959- )
:  .  Christopher George Kennedy (1963- )
:  .  Matthew Maxwell Taylor Kennedy (1965- )
:  .  Douglas Harriman Kennedy (1967- )
:  .  Rory Elizabeth Katherine Kennedy (1968- )
:  Jean Ann Kennedy (1928- )
:  +Stephen Edward Smith (1927- )
:  .  Stephen Edward Smith Jr. (1957- )
:  .  William Kennedy Smith (1960- )
:  .  Amanda Mary Smith (1967- )
:  .  Kym Marie Smith (1972- )
:  Edward Moore Kennedy (1932- )
:  +Virginia Joan Bennett (1936- )
:  .  Kara Ann Kennedy (1960- )
:  .  Edward Moore Kennedy Jr. (1961- )
:  .  Patrick Joseph Kennedy (1967- )
```

The above chart shows each generation indented and the spouse of a descendant is shown with a plus sign.

Family Group Sheets

Family group sheets were the standard tool of genealogists before the invention of the personal computer. Each page contains the vital information about one nuclear family: the husband's name and vital information, the wife's name and vital information, and the names and dates of birth of their children. If a child later married, a new family group sheet is created with the information about that new family. If a person had two or more spouses during a lifetime, two or more family group sheets are created, one for each couple. However, most genealogists will start a new sheet only if the couple had children.

It is not necessary for the couple to be married in order to record information on a family group sheet. A family group sheet makes no moral judgment about legitimate versus illegitimate children. It's simply a method of recording historical facts.

The family group sheet is a very compact method of recording information. Before the introduction of home computers, these sheets were the primary record keeping tools and were preserved in notebooks. Most biographical material, family stories and anecdotes, as well as references to sources of the data, were normally recorded on the reverse side of the family group sheet. However, the genealogist who uses a computer normally will enter that information directly into the computer and will use family group sheets for temporary record keeping only.

What Is a Second Cousin Once Removed?

The chart on page 22 illustrates *cousin relationships*. It may appear confusing at first but if you study it for a bit a pattern will appear. All cousins are descended from a common ancestor, the individual in the top left box. Follow the path of descent for one individual down the left-most column and the path of the other

→ ## A family group sheet

Family Group Sheet

Husband: Joseph Patrick Kennedy	
Born: September 06, 1888	in: East Boston, Suffolk Co, MA
Married: October 07, 1914	in: Boston, Suffolk Co, MA
Died: November 18, 1969	in: Hyannis Port, Barnstable Co, MA
Father: Patrick Joseph Kennedy	
Mother: Mary Augusta Hickey	

Wife: Rose Elizabeth Fitzgerald	
Born: July 22, 1890	in: Boston, Suffolk Co, MA
Died: 1995	
Father: John Francis 'Honey Fitz' Fitzgerald	
Mother: Mary Josephine Hannon	

	CHILDREN	
1 M	Name: Joseph Patrick Kennedy Jr. Born: July 25, 1915 Died: August 12, 1944	in: Hull, Plymouth Co, MA in: the air, Suffolk, England
2 M	Name: John Fitzgerald Kennedy Born: May 29, 1917 Married: September 12, 1953 Died: November 22, 1963 Spouse: Jacqueline Lee Bouvier	in: Brookline, Norfolk Co, MA in: Newport, Newport Co, RI in: Dallas, Dallas Co, TX
3 F	Name: Rosemary (Rose Marie) Kennedy Born: February 20, 1920	in: Brookline, Norfolk Co, MA
4 F	Name: Kathleen 'Kick' Kennedy Born: February 20, 1920 Married: May 06, 1944 Died: May 13, 1948 Spouse: William John Robert Cavendish	in: Brookline, Norfolk Co, MA in: London, England in: Ste-Bauzille, Ardeche, France
5 F	Name: Eunice Mary Kennedy Born: July 10, 1921 Married: May 23, 1953 Spouse: Robert Sargent Shriver Jr.	in: Brookline, Norfolk Co, MA in: New York City, NY
6 F	Name: Patricia Kennedy Born: May 06, 1924 Married: April 24, 1954 Spouse: Peter Lawford	in: Brookline, Norfolk Co, MA in: New York City, NY
7 M	Name: Robert Francis Kennedy Born: November 20, 1925 Married: June 17, 1950 Died: June 06, 1968 Spouse: Ethel Skakel	in: Brookline, Norfolk Co, MA in: Greenwich, Fairfield Co, CT in: Los Angeles, Los Angeles Co, CA
8 F	Name: Jean Ann Kennedy Born: February 20, 1928 Married: May 19, 1956 Spouse: Stephen Edward Smith	in: Boston, Suffolk Co, MA in: New York City, NY
9 M	Name: Edward Moore Kennedy Born: February 22, 1932 Married: November 30, 1958 Spouse: Virginia Joan Bennett	in: Boston, Suffolk Co, MA in: Bronxville, Westchester Co, NY

person across the top row until their relationships with the common ancestor are found. Then follow that row and that column until they intersect in a box within the chart. That indicates their relationship.

Cousin Relationships

Common Ancestor	Child	Grand-child	gGrand-child	ggGrand-child	ggg-Grand-child	gggg-Grand-child	ggggg-Grand-child
Child	Sibling	Niece or Nephew	Grand Niece or Great Nephew	Great Grand Niece or Nephew	ggGrand Niece or Nephew	ggg-Grand Niece or Nephew	gggg-Grand Niece or Nephew
Grand-child	Niece or Nephew	1st Cousin	1st Cousin Once Removed	1st Cousin Twice Removed	1st Cousin Three Times Removed	1st Cousin Four Times Removed	1st Cousin Five Times Removed
gGrand-child	Grand Niece or Great Nephew	1st Cousin Once Removed	Second Cousin	Second Cousin Once Removed	Second Cousin Twice Removed	Second Cousin Three Times Removed	Second Cousin Four Times Removed
ggGrand-child	Great Grand Niece or Nephew	1st Cousin Twice Removed	Second Cousin Once Removed	Third Cousin	Third Cousin Once Removed	Third Cousin Twice Removed	Third Cousin Three Times Removed
ggg-Grand-child	ggGrand Niece or Nephew	1st Cousin Three Times Removed	Second Cousin Twice Removed	Third Cousin Once Removed	Fourth Cousin	Fourth Cousin Once Removed	Fourth Cousin Twice Removed

Cousin Relationships (Continued)

gggg-Grand-child	ggg-Grand Niece or Nephew	1st Cousin Four Times Removed	Second Cousin Three Times Removed	Third Cousin Twice Removed	Fourth Cousin Once Removed	Fifth Cousin	Fifth Cousin Once Removed
ggggg-Grand-child	gggg-Grand Niece or Nephew	1st Cousin Five Times Removed	Second Cousin Four Times Removed	Third Cousin Three Times Removed	Fourth Cousin Twice Removed	Fifth Cousin Once Removed	Sixth Cousin

For instance, let's say that James Smith and William Smith share a *common ancestor* named John Smith. James is the grandson of John, while William is the great-great-grandson of the same John Smith. Since John Smith is the common ancestor, he will be listed in the top left box. Counting down for James's line of descent, we go two boxes and stop, as James is the grandson of the common ancestor. Now do the same for William. Start in the top left corner for the common ancestor and then go across until you find great-great-grandchild as that is William's relationship to the common ancestor. Now find the point at which these two intersect. James and William are *first cousins twice removed*.

Soundex Chart

When you encounter U.S. census records or immigration records, you will frequently find the term *Soundex*. Many old records are indexed by Soundex in order to quickly find family names even when the spelling of the last name varied. In the nineteenth century and earlier, the majority of people did not know how to read or write or even how to spell their own names. Records kept by public officials, ministers, priests, and teachers often used variant spellings. Each person wrote what he or she thought was correct.

At times your more literate ancestors even changed the spellings themselves. The legendary Kentucky trapper and explorer Daniel Boone often spelled his own name as Boone, Boon, or Bone. He was even known to spell it two different ways on the same piece of paper. The inventor of Levi jeans often switched back and forth between Levi and Levy. Most families have similar spelling variations in early generations. While the spellings vary widely, they usually are very close in sound.

Soundex is a major tool for use by the genealogist. In the 1930s the Works Projects Administration (WPA) managed a Federal Works Project in which names and other data on persons enumerated in the censuses of 1880, 1900, part of 1910, and all of 1920 were copied onto file cards. Each of these cards was sorted by Soundex Code. Many immigration records have also had Soundex indexes created and Soundex is now used in computer databases to find possible relatives with similar sounding surnames.

If you are familiar with Soundex codes you can often find family names that were spelled in various ways. For instance, the names Eastman, Eastmen, Estman, Eastmann, and Eastmond all have a Soundex Code of E235 and would be grouped together in Soundex indexes. The same is true of Boone, Boon, and Bone with a Soundex Code of B500. Even Theriault and Terriolt would be grouped together with Soundex T643 even though they might be separated by several pages in a large alphabetical index.

The Soundex filing system consists of an alphabetic character for the first letter of the surname and three numeric characters thereafter. This keeps together names of the same and similar sounds but of variant spellings. To search for a particular name, you must first work out the code number for the surname of the individual. No number is assigned to the first letter of the surname. If the name is Kuhne, for example, the index card will be in the *K* segment of the index. The code number for Kuhne, worked out according to the system below, is K500.

Soundex Coding Guide

Code	Key Letters and Equivalents
1	b, p, f, v
2	c, s, k, g, j, q, x, z
3	d, t
4	l

Code	Key Letters and Equivalents
5	m, n
6	r

The first letter of a surname is *not* coded. Instead, it is listed as the first character of the Soundex code. The letters a, e, i, o, u, y, w, and h are *not* coded. Every Soundex code must be a single letter followed by a three-digit number. A name yielding no code numbers, as Lee, would thus be L000; one yielding only one code number would have two zeros added, as Kuhne, coded as K500; and one yielding two code numbers would have one zero added, as Ebell, coded as E140. Not more than three digits are used, so Ebelson would be coded as E142, not E1425. When two key letters or equivalents appear together, or one key letter immediately follows or precedes an equivalent, the two are coded as one letter, by a single number, as follows: Kelly, coded as K400; Buerck, coded as B620; Lloyd, coded as L300; and Schaefer, coded as S160.

Such prefixes to surnames as *van, Von, Di, de, le, D', dela*, or *du* are usually disregarded in alphabetizing and in coding.

GEDCOM

In the early days of genealogy software, changing from one program to another was very difficult. If 1,000 people were recorded in one program's database, there was no method of transferring that data to a newly purchased genealogy program without typing it all in again. Similarly, if two different people were researching the same family lines but were using different genealogy programs, the only method of sharing data was to print the information on paper from one program and then manually type the data into the second program.

The Mormons have a strong interest in recording genealogy data in computer databases. The Church's Family History Library in Salt Lake City held a conference with other genealogy software developers and from that conference a standardized file format was developed. This file format is called *GEDCOM* which is an abbreviation of: **GE**nealogy **D**ata **COM**munications. All vital information on each individual in a genealogy database is collected and put into a format the receiving computer will understand.

By using GEDCOM, it is now possible to create a file with one genealogy program and then to read that file into a different program. This can even happen between genealogy programs on different operating systems. It's easy to create a GEDCOM file with a Windows genealogy program and then to import that file into a Macintosh genealogy program. However, this standard exists only between genealogy programs that were written to handle GEDCOM. There is no standard for importing dBASE files or Microsoft Excel files or other formats from the popular database or spreadsheet programs.

GEDCOM is still an evolving standard and often lags behind the new features being added to modern genealogy programs. Also, some data fields may exist in the database of one program but not in another which may create problems when transferring data. For instance, one genealogy program allows one database field called "occupation" for each individual. A more sophisticated program allows multiple occupations per person under the assumption that a person may change occupations one or more times during a lifetime. Many of the simpler genealogy programs do not have an occupation field at all. Transferring data from one program to another may result in loss of the occupation entries in the database. There are other pieces of dissimilar information that may be lost as well such as tombstone data, military records, education information, and so on.

Almost all genealogy programs do have a method of tracking data that is not transferred properly when reading a GEDCOM file into the database. When importing GEDCOM files, most genealogy programs will create a file called ERROR.LOG or a similar name. Each piece of information in the GEDCOM file that cannot be placed into the database is written to the ERROR.LOG file. The user can then later read the entries in this log and then manually enter the data into the new database into the fields that seem to be the most appropriate. This may require a lot of manual clean-up work but is still much easier than typing everything in manually!

While GEDCOM is not a perfect method of transferring data, it does almost always transfer the vital information of name, dates and places of birth, marriage and death, etc. You should make sure that any genealogy program you are considering purchasing can read and write GEDCOM files. There are GEDCOM-compatible programs available today for MS-DOS, Windows, Macintosh, Amiga, Atari, and Unix. All genealogy programs discussed in this book have full GEDCOM support.

Tiny Tafel

Tiny Tafel is a method of providing a compact way of describing a family database so that the information can be scanned visually or by computer. It was first described in an article entitled *Tiny Tafel for Database Scope Indexing*, by Paul Andereck in the April-May-June 1986 (Vol 5, No.4) issue of *Genealogical Computing* magazine. The format proposed was for a "tiny ahnentafel" or Tiny Tafel for short.

In 1986 the typical high-end home computer was an XT clone with 640K of memory and two floppy-disk drives with a purchase price of about $2,500. Commodore 64, TRS-80, and Apple II computers were much more popular among hobbyists than the more expensive MS-DOS systems. Very few hobbyists could afford the "huge" 20MB hard drives of the time because that added another $600 or so to the purchase price. Online communications were normally conducted at either 300 or 1,200 baud.

The concept advanced in the magazine article was that computers could be used to find other genealogists who were interested in the same surnames and locations. The idea suggested was to create databases of surnames along with information on who was interested in each one. Since the required storage space to hold everyone's interests was prohibitively expensive at that time, the article proposed a new abbreviated list that was compact and could be read either by the human eye or by computer programs. By making the Tiny Tafel files as small as possible, hundreds of them could be squeezed onto a floppy disk and thousands could be stored on the typical hard drives of 1986.

The concept of Tiny Tafels was first implemented by CommSoft, Inc. in their popular genealogy program, Roots-II, and then in their later versions Roots-III and Roots-IV. It has since been adopted by two shareware programs: Brother's Keeper and Family ScrapBook. However, Tiny Tafel has never become popular in the other leading genealogy programs. Several small utility programs have appeared that generate Tiny Tafel files, but these are not full-fledged genealogy database programs.

CommSoft initially sponsored a network of bulletin board systems running the "Tafel Matching System" software. The software was provided by CommSoft and the "hub" bulletin board system was established at their corporate offices. A small network of dial-up bulletin board systems (BBSs) was soon established around the country with each BBS containing a Tiny Tafel database obtained from local users. These BBSs were owned and operated by those individuals with the interest and the finances to provide a dedicated PC with a 40MB or so disk drive. A genealogist could dial into one of these BBSs and send a Tiny Tafel file for matching. Over a period of time each BBS would connect to other, similar systems and compare that Tiny Tafel file with other Tiny Tafel files stored in the various systems. Once the Tafel Matching System network was in place it was possible to submit a file and to receive a matching report about a week later.

As prices for hard drive storage dropped and as communication speeds increased, other online systems with national and international access became available to genealogists. CommSoft stopped running the Tafel Matching Software on their BBS in 1990 but some privately owned systems continue to use the same software even today.

Online systems now routinely use 14,400 baud communications and contain disk drives in the gigabyte range. However, the Tiny Tafel format remains popular as a method of quickly listing surnames of interest along with minimal information about dates and places. One MS-DOS program, Tiny Tafel Editor, written by Christopher Long, allows for storing your own Tiny Tafel file along with hundreds of others on your local hard-disk drive and quickly matching your surname interests against those of hundreds of others. Collections of Tiny Tafel files are available for downloading from several of the online services allowing the genealogist to quickly obtain hundreds of Tiny Tafel files for comparison purposes. Matching reports are now available within minutes instead of the days or weeks previously required.

Tiny Tafel Editor can be obtained online from CompuServe's Genealogy Forum and from most other online services. It is an MS-DOS shareware program supported by its author on several online services.

A Tiny Tafel file makes no attempt to include the details that are included in a normal ahnentafel. It only lists surnames of interest (with Soundex Code) plus the locations and dates of the beginning and end of that surname. Tiny Tafels make no provision for first names, births, marriages, deaths, or for multiple locations. All data fields are fixed length for easy parsing by software with the obvious exceptions of the surnames and the optional places names.

Here's an excerpt from the Tiny Tafel file of another famous American:

```
N George Herbert Walker Bush
A Houston, TX
Z 190 BUSH V33 SDMP
A215 1762 1822 Aspinwall
A360 1714 1714 Adair\Down, Ireland/Down, Ireland
A450 1561 1591 Allen
A450 1637 1637 Allen
A524 1680 1680 Angell
A654 1587 1617 Arnold\England
B200 1758 1841 Bechi,Beaky/Emmitsburg, MD
B200 1705 1954 Bush
B255 1623 1693 Beekman
B260 1673 1703 Bocher\Germany/Germany
B346 1696 1850 Butler/Columbus, OH
B400 1701 1701 Ball
B420 1681 1681 Bullock\Rehoboth, MA/Rehoboth, MA
B424 1531 1681 Bulkeley
      (and so on)
```

You'll quickly notice that each surname is limited to only two locations: the earliest known and the last locations. If a family migrated every two or three generations all the in-between locations are ignored.

Unlike an ahnentafel, the format of the Tiny Tafel is rigidly controlled so that the data may be read by computers. Here's the specification as released by CommSoft:

Header Column	Description
1	Header type
2	Space delimiter
3 - n	Text (n < 38)
(n + 1)	Carriage Return

Defined Types:

Header Type	Description	Remarks
N	Name of person having custody of data	Mandatory first record
A	Address data, 0 to 5 address lines	Optional
T	Telephone number including area code	Optional
S	Communication Service (CompuServe, Prodigy, BBS, and so on) 0 to 5 lines	Optional
B	Bulletin Board/telephone number	Optional
C	Communications nnnn/X/P where nnnn = maximum baud rate, X = O(riginate only), A(nswer only), B(oth), P = Protocol (Xmodem, Kermit, and so on)	Optional
D	Disk format d/f/c where d = diameter (3, 5, 8), f = format MS-DOS, Macintosh, and so on, c = capacity in kilobytes	Optional
F	File format: ROOTS II, ROOTS/M, PAF Version 1, and so on	Free-form, optional
R	Remark	Free-form, optional
Z	Number of data items with optional text	Required last item

Tiny Tafel Data:

Code	Key Letters and Equivalents
1 through 4	Soundex Code[1]
5	Space delimiter
6 through 9	Earliest ancestor birth year
10	Interest flag, ancestor end of family line[2]
11 through 14	Latest descendant birth year
15	Interest flag, descendant end of family line[2]
16 through 16+SL	Surname string area (SL = total surname length)[3]

Code	Key Letters and Equivalents
above + PL	Place name area (PL = total place name length)[4]
above + 1	Carriage return

[1] The Soundex code for any given line is obtained from the end of the line that has the highest interest level. If interest level is the same at each end, however, the name at the ancestor end will be used. If the application of these rules yield a surname that cannot be converted to Soundex, however, the program will attempt to obtain a Soundex code from the other end of the line.

[2] Interest flag:

[space]	No interest (level 0)
.	Low interest (level 1)
:	Moderate interest (level 2)
*	Highest interest (level 3)

[3] Up to five surnames can be accommodated for one line where surname has changed in that line. If more than five surnames are found in a line, only the latest five will be shown. The inclusion of additional surnames is enabled by the M switch.

[4] Place names for the birth of the earliest ancestor and the latest descendant may be included by using the P switch. If a place name is not provided for the individual whose birth year is shown, the field will be blank. The place for the ancestor is preceded by a backslash (\) and for the descendant by a slash (/).

Terminator:

W   Date Tiny Tafel file was generated, DD MMM YYYY format.

Despite the fact that most genealogy programs will not create Tiny Tafel files, these files are popular on many online services.

What to Keep Track Of

Now that you are familiar with the basic terminology used in computerized genealogy, you are in a better position to decide what information you want to record. You now know the genealogist's "tools of the trade" and have an idea of how to record information. You should be familiar with basic paper forms even if you enter everything directly into a computer. You should select a genealogy program that allows for the recording of conflicting data, such as multiple dates of birth, marriage, or death, or even spelling differences in names. The genealogy program you select should allow for the recording of *sources* of information as well as the stated facts. You will always want to record not only information about a person or an event but also will record where you obtained that data. The genealogy program you choose should also support GEDCOM file format so that you can easily import and export data to share with others.

A small investment in time and effort at the beginning of your genealogy research will simplify your later work.

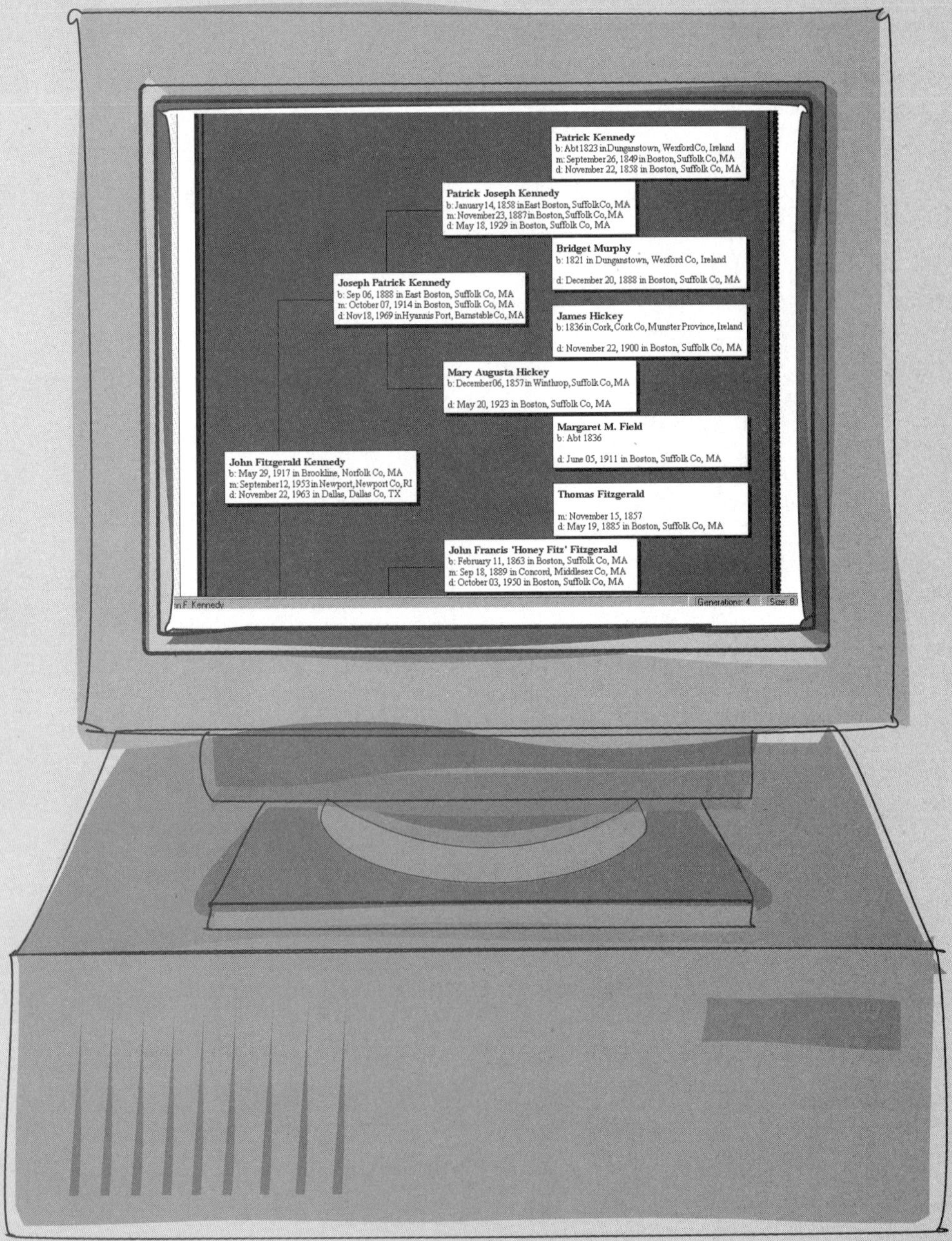
Patrick Kennedy
b: Abt 1823 in Dunganstown, Wexford Co, Ireland
m: September 26, 1849 in Boston, Suffolk Co, MA
d: November 22, 1858 in Boston, Suffolk Co, MA
Patrick Joseph Kennedy
b: January 14, 1858 in East Boston, Suffolk Co, MA
m: November 23, 1887 in Boston, Suffolk Co, MA
d: May 18, 1929 in Boston, Suffolk Co, MA
Bridget Murphy
b: 1821 in Dunganstown, Wexford Co, Ireland
d: December 20, 1888 in Boston, Suffolk Co, MA
Joseph Patrick Kennedy
b: Sep 06, 1888 in East Boston, Suffolk Co, MA
m: October 07, 1914 in Boston, Suffolk Co, MA
d: Nov 18, 1969 in Hyannis Port, Barnstable Co, MA
James Hickey
b: 1836 in Cork, Cork Co, Munster Province, Ireland
d: November 22, 1900 in Boston, Suffolk Co, MA
Mary Augusta Hickey
b: December 06, 1857 in Winthrop, Suffolk Co, MA
d: May 20, 1923 in Boston, Suffolk Co, MA
Margaret M. Field
b: Abt 1836
d: June 05, 1911 in Boston, Suffolk Co, MA
John Fitzgerald Kennedy
b: May 29, 1917 in Brookline, Norfolk Co, MA
m: September 12, 1953 in Newport, Newport Co, RI
d: November 22, 1963 in Dallas, Dallas Co, TX
Thomas Fitzgerald
m: November 15, 1857
d: May 19, 1885 in Boston, Suffolk Co, MA
John Francis 'Honey Fitz' Fitzgerald
b: February 11, 1863 in Boston, Suffolk Co, MA
m: Sep 18, 1889 in Concord, Middlesex Co, MA
d: October 03, 1950 in Boston, Suffolk Co, MA
Generations: 4

3

What Do I Need to **Get** Started?

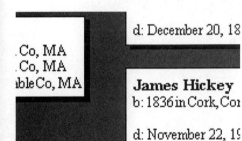

Genealogy

Genealogy has been a popular hobby for over a century and obviously computers weren't used in "the old days." Of course it is possible to find information about your ancestors and to record it without ever touching a computer—many thousands of people have done just that. But by using today's technology you can speed and simplify the process greatly. You can spend a few hours searching CD-ROM databases or recording and organizing information obtained in a modern genealogy program and thereby accomplish more than you could in several months without using a computer.

Today's genealogy programs allow you to copy large amounts of information directly from CD-ROM databases without retyping. You can exchange information with distant relatives by disk or by modem. The new information may be placed directly into your database if you wish. Information is easily updated as new facts are discovered.

CD-ROM databases of census records, the Mormons's databases, old genealogy books converted to computerized text, and various other sources are now available with new ones appearing every year. You can compare notes and obtain assistance from other genealogists around the world quickly and easily by computer. Perhaps best of all, you can publish all this information in some genealogy programs that rival desktop publishing systems in their ability to organize and print information and graphics. The genealogists of only a few years ago would be envious of the tools available today.

Windows, MS-DOS, OS/2, or Macintosh?

There are more than 50 genealogy programs available today; the majority of them are designed for use with MS-DOS or Windows. In fact, the most powerful genealogy programs available today are MS-DOS programs. However, all this is changing quickly as new and more powerful Windows genealogy programs are appearing in the marketplace constantly. The new programs for Windows are generally much easier to use, primarily because of the consistency the Windows interface brings to programs. Also, the Windows genealogy programs allow the developers to easily include scanned graphics, sophisticated printouts, plotter-generated charts, and even sound clips with less programming effort, as the Windows drivers for these already exist. All of the MS-DOS and Windows genealogy programs perform well under OS/2. In fact, some people report they run better under OS/2 than in their original environments.

The programs that are available today vary widely in hardware requirements. Some MS-DOS programs, such as *Brothers Keeper*, will run on an old XT-compatible computer with only 640K of RAM memory and a rather small hard drive. The more powerful MS-DOS genealogy programs, such as *The Master Genealogist* and *Roots IV*, will demand more from the hardware. Both of these systems require at least an 80386 system with 4MB of memory, but the best performance is obtained with 8MB of memory or more. Disk space can also be quickly soaked up by these powerhouses. The exact size obviously depends upon the amount of information that you wish to store in your personal database, but plan for at least 20MB to hold the programs and the data. The Windows genealogy programs will require the same hardware as the more powerful MS-DOS programs: an 80386 with at least 4MB of memory. Again, a more powerful system will run faster.

Macintosh owners should not feel left out. While there are fewer Macintosh genealogy programs available, they are just as good as their Windows competitors. Genealogy programs on the Mac are generally as easy to use as any other Macintosh program. We will later examine the most powerful Macintosh genealogy program available today. Any Macintosh capable of running a modern word processing program or spreadsheet program will have plenty of capacity for today's genealogy programs.

In short, anyone with a Macintosh, a modern PC running Windows or OS/2, or even an older PC running MS-DOS will find high-quality genealogy software available today. This book will examine the more popular MS-DOS, Windows, and Macintosh genealogy programs in depth.

Selecting Software

With all the genealogy software available today, the most common question is "Which one is best for me?" While there is no quick and easy answer, the next few pages will describe the leading programs available for Windows, MS-DOS, and Macintosh, and describe each in some detail. These programs are all well-established in the marketplace and are supported by their producers online as well as by telephone support. Each of these programs has thousands of users worldwide.

Each of the genealogy programs detailed here supports GEDCOM files. GED-COM is an abbreviation for *Genealogy Data COM*munications, a more or less standardized format for exchanging data files between different genealogy programs. It is possible to create a GEDCOM file in any of these programs and then later translate it into any of the other programs listed here. You may even exchange genealogy databases between a Macintosh and a PC this way. GEDCOM is not only useful for sharing files with others, it can also be used to transfer your own data from one genealogy program to another. It is also the format used to obtain data from the CD-ROM discs produced by the Church of Jesus Christ of Latter-day Saints (the Mormons).

GEDCOM is not a perfect standard yet and not all data is guaranteed to transfer properly. Different genealogy programs may store data in different ways so some loss of details may occur. All of these programs will import names as well as dates and places of birth, marriage, and death properly. Details such as military service, occupations, tombstone inscriptions, and so forth may not transfer into a program that doesn't have database fields for that information. All of these genealogy programs keep error logs when importing GEDCOM data and those logs will show the data that was not handled properly. You can then go back and manually insert the information that did not transfer automatically.

Windows Genealogy Programs

Family Origins for Windows Produced by Parsons Technology, this easy-to-use genealogy program has advanced features not often seen in its price range. It is an enhanced version of an earlier MS-DOS version of Family Origins which is still available. Family Origins for Windows may be purchased directly from Parsons Technology as well as in many retail stores. The exact price will depend upon the discounts offered, but you should be able to find Family Origins for Windows for $30 or perhaps a bit less in discount stores.

Data entry into Family Origins is straightforward and intuitive at all times. The program will automatically link family members' relationships together as data is entered, and errors in data entry are easily corrected. Each database may contain up to 30,000 individuals and the program allows for up to 255 different databases in each subdirectory and then multiple subdirectories may be used for even more databases. Among the features of Family Origins for Windows are

- ➡ Notes Editor—can be used to record anecdotes, personal information, and other biographical information. Family Origins allows you to enter a note for every person, event, or marriage. Notes may be entered any time you are in a data entry screen (either individual or marriage) by pressing Alt-N. A note editor will appear for you to enter your note. If the cursor is in an event field (date or place) when you press Alt-N, you may enter a note for that event. Each event note may contain up to 1,200 characters. If the cursor is not in an event field when you press Alt-N, you may enter an "individual" or "marriage" note. An "individual" or "marriage" note may contain up to 20,000 characters.

- ➡ Tracking of information specific to the whole family—such as: genetic diseases, births of twins or triplets, and so on.

- ➡ Full support for scanned photos and other graphics—you can have a picture for each person in your database.

- ➡ A powerful Relationship Calculator—quickly determines blood relationship between any two individuals in the database. This will end the confusion about "second cousin, twice removed" as the program will calculate that automatically.

- ➡ A large number of printed reports—including pedigree charts, ahnentafel charts, descendant charts, ancestor charts, family group records, Register Format Reports, and so on. You can also produce reports of statistics such as average age at time of death or at time of marriage.

- ➡ GEDCOM file import and export capability—plus the ability to import files from Personal Ancestral File, an older MS-DOS program produced by the Mormons and at one time a very popular genealogy program.

➡ Merge capability—allows the merging of records from two or more databases. This is useful if you have two different records which contain information for the same person.

➡ Photographs—Family Origins allows you to attach scanned images to any individual in your database. You can also print the images to your printer.

➡ ## Family Origins for Windows Pedigree Chart

Moving around this chart is easily done with the mouse, simply point and click. The "base individual" is always shown at the extreme left of the screen, in this case John F. Kennedy.

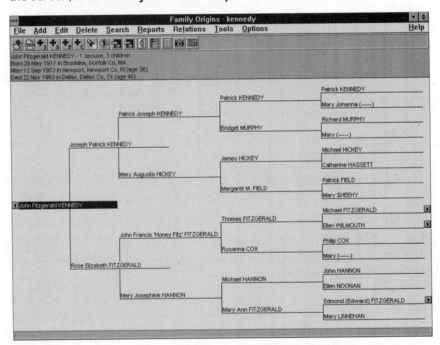

The Edit Individual screen accepts all the normal vital statistics of birth, christening, death, burial, and so on. In addition, up to three User Defined fields may be added for those events the programmer didn't think of. Also, notice the Note and Source buttons in the bottom of the Edit Individual window; clicking on them opens up still more windows for recording biographical information and recording the sources of the information obtained.

Double-clicking on an individual produces a fill-in window of detailed information.

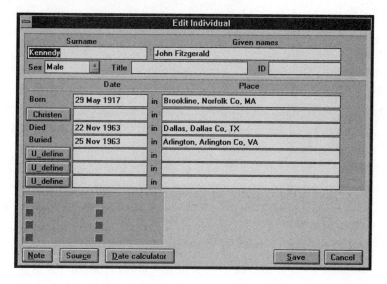

Family Origins for Windows also has an excellent Date Calculator that quickly calculates years, months, and days, or converts that information back to original dates. For instance, a tombstone may read "Died Jan. 23, 1842, at the age of 78 years, 5 months, 28 days." A quick check with Family Origins' Date Calculator shows the birthdate to be July 26, 1763.

Backups One of the greatest hazards a genealogist can encounter with a computer is the sudden loss of data representing many hours' work. In the computer world, backups are necessary but often overlooked. Family Origins for Windows has a built-in backup routine that simplifies the process. The File Backup command is used to make compressed backup files on a floppy disk. The program first will ask you which drive and directory you want to send the backup to. Then Family Origins will compress all the files in the current database as it backs them up, so the backup will use much less disk space than the original database. The backup that Family Origins creates will be an executable program. If you need to restore your database from the backup, just run the program that Family Origins creates, and it will extract your backed up database.

Reports Family Origins for Windows creates many different reports, including Pedigree Charts, Family Group Sheets, Descendancy Charts (lists of descendants), Ancestor Charts (ahnentafels), Individual Summaries, and Family Summaries. One thing unique to Family Origins is the Statistics Report which prints various statistics (such as average age at death) for individuals in your database. The selection screen will appear and allow you to select the individuals you want included in the report.

Another excellent report is simply called "Problems." This is the potential problem report which analyzes the entire database and creates a report which lists potential data entry problems (for example, individuals with a death date occurring before their birth date, births after the mother's death, and so on).

Family Origins for Windows will also print complete genealogy books in Modified Register format, producing a complete book of the descendants of one person. This feature is unusual in a $30 genealogy program and makes Family Origins for Windows one of the most powerful programs for the money.

Numerous "lists" may be printed, such as:

- Unlinked Individuals—List of all people not linked to anyone
- Index of People—List of all people and the personal data entered
- Duplicate List—List of possible duplicate records
- Notes and Sources—Individual Sources prints the individual notes for the highlighted person, Family Sources prints the marriage notes for the highlighted person
- Ordinances (LDS) Entry Forms—Individual and marriage submission forms for LDS ordinances as used by the Mormons

Finally, you can create Custom Reports to meet your own needs. After selecting "Reports Custom," a report design screen will appear. The design screen is divided into three sections: Title, Header, and Body.

➡ Title—Prints at the top of the first page of the report. Special characters: @ will turn into current date, # will become page number, | justifies title parts. Example: a|b|c : a is left justified, b is centered, c is right justified.

➡ Header—Prints at the top of every page and is followed by a line. Same special characters as Title are allowed.

➡ Body—Prints for every record in the report. The body section of the report layout screen is where the meat of the report is defined. When the cursor is in the body section, you can press Alt-F to add a new field. A pick list of all available fields will appear. Family Origins will place the field you select at the current cursor position. You may then use the mouse to drag the field to the desired position, or hold down the Ctrl key while moving the mouse to size the field.

To delete a field, move the cursor anywhere into the field, and press the Delete key.

The following items let you select other report characteristics:

➡ Load report—lets you load a report definition from the disk

➡ Save report—lets you save the current report definition

➡ Move/Size field—lets you move or size a field using the arrow keys

➡ Sort field—order to sort the individuals in the report by

➡ Blank rows between records—number of rows to separate each record

➡ Alt-P—select the people and print the report

All printouts can be made in a wide variety of fonts.

Family Origins includes a rather slim user's manual of 50 pages plus an index. Since the program is intuitive and easy to use, that small book will suffice for most users. Another booklet included with the program is Alice Eicholz's *Discovering Your Heritage*. This explains the basics of researching your family origins and will help you get started in your search.

Family Origins for Windows is an excellent program for the money, combining an easy-to-use Windows interface and printed reports often not available in more expensive genealogy programs. A demo version of Family Origins for Windows is on the CD-ROM disc included with this book.

Family Tree Maker for Windows This program from Banner Blue Software is available in two versions: The regular version which is installed from floppy disks, and a deluxe version available on CD-ROM. The two programs are virtually identical and each one can keep up to two million people in its database. The deluxe version of Family Tree Maker for Windows (often abbreviated FTW) includes an index of 100 million names from the U.S. Census Records. This is the only genealogy program available today that comes bundled with such a database. The same CD-ROM disc also contains an excellent "Genealogy 'How-To' Guide" that offers a lot of guidance for the genealogy newcomer. You do not need to leave the CD-ROM disc in the computer after installing Family Tree Maker Deluxe Edition, as all the normal program files are copied to your hard disk. You will need to insert the CD-ROM only when searching the 100 million names index or when using the "Genealogy 'How-To' Guide."

Prices for Family Tree Maker vary from store to store; the floppy disk version can normally be obtained for $30 to $40. The Family Tree Maker for Windows Deluxe CD-ROM Edition will sell for about $70 in discount stores. This price includes a very detailed user's manual that is more than 400 pages.

Working with Family Tree Maker for Windows is always intuitive; the company has obviously spent a lot of time designing an interface that is easy to use. While the thick user's manual does explain operations in detail, it usually is not needed. Among the features of FTW are

➡ FamilyFinder Index (available in the CD-ROM version only)—Many of the records that you use for genealogical research, such as census records and marriage records, have been indexed on CD-ROM discs. These indexes can help you save time by telling you exactly where to go to get the record that you are searching for. The CD-ROM version of Family Tree Maker for Windows comes equipped with the FamilyFinder Index. This index is a "Super Index" to existing archives. The FamilyFinder Index contains the names of approximately 100 million individuals that appear in U.S. census records, selected state marriage records, selected state land records, all publicly available Social Security death benefits records, and many other archives. The FamilyFinder Index is an index of actual names. It can tell you within seconds exactly where to go to

Family Tree Maker for Windows

FTW allows a choice of "default screens" to work from. The more popular one is called the Family Page which looks like a card file.

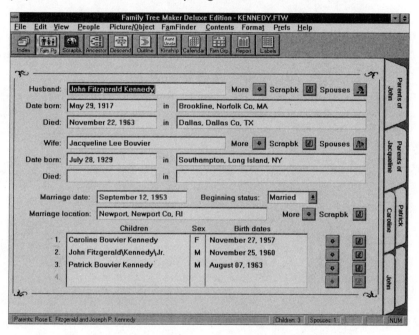

obtain more detailed information about each listed person. However, the index only points to the existence of a name on another CD-ROM disc that must be purchased separately. The actual data is not on the Family Tree Maker for Windows CD-ROM.

Printed Reports—Family Tree Maker for Windows probably has the best looking printouts available in genealogy programs today. The reports available include pedigree charts, family group sheets, calendars showing birthdays and anniversaries in any given month, Kinship Reports (showing who is a "second cousin, twice removed" and so on) as well as the ability to display some limited "custom reports" that are lists of individuals who meet some user-specified criteria. Family Tree Maker also has the capability of printing most reports to the Windows Clipboard, allowing the

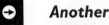 *Another FTW view is the Ancestor Page.*

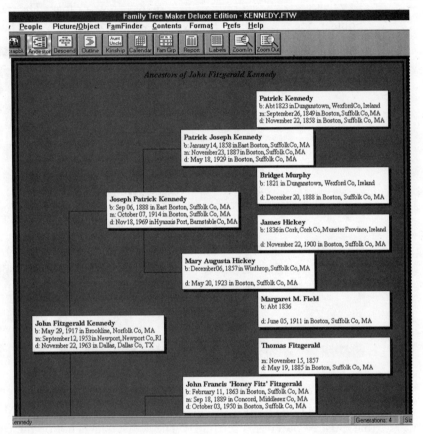

reports to then be pasted into almost any Windows programs such as a word processor.

One very useful reporting capability in FTW is the ability to print on Avery gummed labels and cards. This is useful for making mailing labels, name tags, rolling index cards, address book pages, or even postcards to be mailed as invitations to a family reunion. Family Tree Maker for Windows can store mailing addresses for all living individuals in its database and use those addresses in a variety of ways.

Genealogy "How-To" Guide One of the nicest features of Family Tree Maker for Windows Deluxe Edition is a very complete guide for getting started in genealogy. The information is contained on the CD-ROM disc and can be searched quickly. Among the items contained in this guide are

- ➡ Directory of addresses and telephone numbers of major archives, libraries, and genealogy societies around the United States. This includes a list of all the county courthouses in the U.S.
- ➡ Information on various ethnic and religious groups
- ➡ An extensive bibliography of genealogy books
- ➡ Genealogy Dictionary
- ➡ Numerous form letters and blank forms

Among the other features of Family Tree Maker for Windows are

- ➡ Ability to store genetic information and other medical information on each person, allowing for easier tracking of inherited medical conditions
- ➡ Ability to store any type of text information on each individual, such as height, weight, personality, habits, or even favorite recipes
- ➡ Excellent support of scanned photographs and other graphics
- ➡ The ability to use scanned pictures, film clips, sound files, and almost anything else that can be stored as Windows OLE (Object Linking and Embedding) files. Kodak Photo CD pictures may be used in conjunction with FTW. A CD-ROM can be made of your pictures easily and these can be displayed within Family Tree Maker for Windows.
- ➡ The capability of recording the sources of information contained within the database
- ➡ GEDCOM files can easily be imported and exported with FTW's GEDCOM file utility

The program automatically makes backup files every time the user exits from the program. These are placed in a separate subdirectory, but it is up to the user to copy these to disk or tape.

Notes Editor This is one of the more useful features of FTW. It includes a mini-word processor that allows for capturing any useful information about the individual listed. These can be short notes: perhaps information about the personality or accomplishments of the individual, or maybe even his or her favorite foods. Other screens within the Notes Editor allow for the capture of medical information, lineage information, mailing address for living individuals, and the recording of sources of information. You cannot print the information in the normal family tree printouts, but you can print the information on separate pages for easy filing.

Scrapbook Perhaps the most unique feature of FTW is the Scrapbook. Essentially this is the place where the pictures, school papers, film clips, sound clips, and other OLE files are stored and are made available for later use. The Scrapbook may be the most powerful part of Family Tree Maker for Windows. It has an extensive Scrapbook editor that even allows for setting up of complete "multimedia slide shows" that can be played back at any time. The instructions for the Scrapbook alone take up 40 pages in the user's manual that accompanies Family Tree Maker for Windows.

Family Tree Maker for Windows is an excellent program for the money, combining an easy-to-use Windows interface and some of the nicest looking printed reports available anywhere. A demo version of Family Tree Maker for Windows (regular edition) is included on the CD-ROM disc included with this book.

Reunion for Windows Probably the most powerful Windows genealogy program, Reunion by Leister Productions, is for the serious genealogist. It combines the power of your existing favorite word processor along with database and charting software designed for the discriminating genealogist. The program is available in two versions: Macintosh and Windows. The two are similar in concept, although there are considerable differences in details. The Windows version will run on an Intel 286 PC with VGA or better display and at least 2MB of memory. Most users will prefer a 386 or faster computer with at least 4MB of memory.

Although Reunion for Windows has a list price of $169, the program is carried by a number of mail-order discount houses with prices between $99 and $110.

Reunion for Windows stores and displays all the standard genealogy facts along with plenty of notes, sources of information, and digitized pictures. It displays family relationships easily. It creates all the standard genealogy reports such as: person sheets, family group sheets, family histories, pedigree charts, and descendant charts. It also creates birthday calendars, mailing lists, question- naires, and indexes. It can calculate and identify tricky relationships, such as "second cousin twice removed."

Most other genealogy programs create printed reports directly from the pro- gram. While they may have sophisticated reporting capabilities, they rarely match the power of a modern Windows word processor. The ability to have bold text, italics, underlines, boxes, and so on may be limited. Reunion has taken a different approach by utilizing the power of your favorite word processor to cre- ate text reports. Reunion will link together with Microsoft Word, Ami Pro, Word- Perfect, or Windows Write to create reports. The reports are created internally within Reunion and then passed to the word processor which is automatically started for you. You then may edit and add enhancements as you wish to the standard reports. Of course, you can either print these reports immediately or store them for later use on your word processor. This ability to directly integrate your favorite word processor into a genealogy program is unique to Reunion.

One other capability in Reunion not seen in the less expensive programs is the ability to create large, high-resolution graphic charts, including the ability to edit boxes, lines, fonts, and colors. These large charts can be printed in multiple colors on large plotters or they can be printed on regular printers with the result- ant pages taped together. For instance, it is possible to print a multicolor family tree that is 8 feet wide by 8 feet high or even larger. That can be very interesting to take to a family gathering!

Reunion's default screen uses the *stack-of-cards* metaphor. Each card shows in- formation for one immediate family which is called the Family Card. Family Cards are then related and linked together to create extended families. A family card will exist for each couple and unmarried individual in the database. In the case of one person having multiple spouses, different Family Cards are created for each couple. Note that an actual marriage is not required for a Family Card. Use of these Family Cards allows quick and easy navigation throughout family links.

To navigate around Reunion, you click on buttons. Each child has a button— rectangular buttons for sons and oval-shaped buttons for daughters. When you click on a child's button you open the Family Card for that child. If you click on a parent's button, you go to the parent's Family Card. A toolbar is shown along the right-hand edge showing many other tools available at all times.

 ### Reunion for Windows

It is possible to have pictures displayed on screen as well as integrated into reports. For instance, this picture can be displayed while looking at a Family Card.

Reunion also can create a wide variety of charts, such as the descendant chart. Among the charts available in Reunion for Windows are

- Person sheet which lists all the known information about any one person
- Questionnaire which is similar to a person sheet but also shows blanks for missing information. This is excellent for use when interviewing family members
- Descendant Reports up to 99 generations. These can be huge when printed on a plotter or on multiple sheets of paper that are taped together

- ➔ Family Group Sheets in several formats
- ➔ Family History reports that show one couple and then all of their descendants, including all the recorded information about each descendant
- ➔ Mailing Lists that can be used directly as mail merge documents in leading word processors
- ➔ Ages, a special dialog box that computes the exact weekday of birth, death, and marriage dates and the current age of a living person. It also will calculate the life span of a deceased person, the age at marriage, and the length of that marriage.
- ➔ Direct Lines report that displays the chain of people between you and an ancestor
- ➔ Relationships calculator that displays the blood relationship between two people, such as second cousin, twice removed
- ➔ Index report shows an alphabetical list of everyone in the database
- ➔ Calendars can be printed showing birthdays and anniversaries in a given month
- ➔ GEDCOM files may also be imported and exported from Reunion for Windows

Reunion for Windows does an excellent job of combining database capabilities, graphics, and textual information. It creates charts and builds text reports for use by your favorite word processor. It also includes some multimedia capabilities. While Reunion is not a "desktop publishing" program, it comes closer to that than any other genealogy program does. For anyone who is serious about publishing genealogy information, Reunion for Windows is tough to beat. A demo version of Reunion for Windows is included on the CD-ROM disk included with this book.

Windows Shareware

Shareware programs are often referred to as "try before you buy" programs. These programs are made available by the authors on a trial basis. You may legally try a shareware program for a period of time (usually 30 days) to see if you wish to use the program on a regular basis. If you decide to keep and use the program, you are obligated to pay for the program. This is called a "shareware registration fee" and is normally paid directly to the author or via the Shareware Registration service on CompuServe. If you decide that you do not wish to keep the program, you simply delete it from your disk drive and you pay nothing. Shareware distribution gives users a chance to try software before buying it. Shareware is a distribution method, not a type of software. If you try a shareware program and continue using it, you are expected to register.

Shareware is not free software. Copyright laws apply to both shareware and commercial software. In both cases the copyright holder retains all rights. Shareware authors are usually accomplished programmers, just like commercial authors, and the programs may be of comparable quality. (In both cases, there are good programs and bad ones!) The main difference is in the method of distribution.

Shareware programs vary widely. Some are simple programs that will not compete with commercial programs. Other shareware programs may be even more sophisticated and yet cheaper than their commercial cousins. Since you are not under any obligation to pay for the program until after you have used it for a while, your risk is minimal. Shareware has the ultimate money-back guarantee—if you don't use the product, you don't pay for it.

Shareware genealogy programs are available from all of the online services listed elsewhere (except Prodigy) and there are many to choose from. The most popular shareware genealogy program for Windows is *Family Tree for Windows.*

Family Tree for Windows This is a "bare bones" genealogy program that will allow you to accomplish the basics. Family Tree for Windows (FT4WIN) has a database that keeps track of all vital information and allows for multiple reports. It also can import and export GEDCOM files. That allows you to move your data back and forth to other programs to use extended reports at any time. You can use FT4WIN on a trial basis for 30 days. If you decide to keep it the shareware registration fee is $40, which can be paid directly to the author or via the shareware registration (SWREG) area on CompuServe.

Family Tree's clean and easy user interface is based upon a pedigree chart

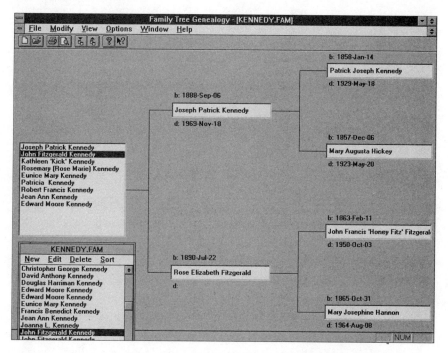

The program can print three types of charts: Pedigree, Family Group Sheets, and a report referred to as "Full Chart." A Full Chart is a pictorial representation of a family group sheet, showing parents, children, and spouses.

The program uses a "click and drag" interface; to find information about a person you click on that individual and hold the button down while moving to the interface wanted. For instance, to see the pedigree of an individual, you first locate that person in the Individual List window, click on him or her and drag that person's name to the pedigree chart. All pertinent information then appears in the chart.

A complete copy of Family Tree for Windows is included on the CD-ROM disc that accompanies this book.

MS-DOS Genealogy Programs

Despite the popularity of Windows and Macintosh systems, the most powerful genealogy programs available today are MS-DOS programs. The producers of the "top three" MS-DOS genealogy programs have all announced that they will be producing a Windows version in the future, but today they are only available in MS-DOS. These high-powered specialty programs are all produced by small specialty software houses that are dedicated full-time to their genealogy programs. These companies often lack the resources to produce multiple versions simultaneously. Instead, they choose to focus their efforts on one main product and that product today is their MS-DOS version. Undoubtedly, this will change soon as user demand for Windows programs increases. We will examine the two most powerful commercial MS-DOS genealogy programs and also the leading shareware program that actually is much more powerful than many commercial programs.

The Master Genealogist This is the newest of the powerful MS-DOS genealogy programs and has many features not found elsewhere. It is produced by a company that is cleverly-named Wholly Genes, Incorporated. The Master Genealogist (or TMG for short) is a very powerful program that stresses research and the meticulous recording of sources and repositories of information. Its recording and quick recall of all details involved in genealogy research will satisfy the most demanding professional genealogist. Yet it has an easy-to-use interface that will appeal to even the novice user. The Master Genealogist is available by mail order for $99.95. A Windows version of TMG has been announced by Wholly Genes, but delivery is not expected for some time.

TMG for MS-DOS requires at least a 386SX computer and 4MB of RAM memory. However, most users will want a higher-speed CPU, and running in 8MB of memory also adds a performance boost.

TMG allows for recording even the most minute details encountered in genealogy research. If you want to record an event or a piece of information that the programmers didn't envision, you can create your own events and tags. Whether you wish to record everything or just the minimal information, TMG will accommodate your wishes. Its menus never get in the way.

Another feature of TMG that is unusual in MS-DOS genealogy programs is its heavy support of scanned graphics and even sound clips. It supports Sound-Blaster files in VOC format. You can even record your own voice as a sound file within TMG and use that as a narration in a "genealogy slide show." TMG supports seven different video formats: BMP, GIF, IMG, PCX, PNT, TIF, and X11.

One feature of TMG that is unique is its implementation of "timelines." These display a person's lifetime along with the events of those years so that you can quickly and easily see what affected your ancestor's life. For instance, you may find that he sold the farm and moved west the year after a great drought. Several timelines are included with The Master Genealogist and you may easily modify these or create new ones. Timelines can reflect major national events such as wars or the election of new presidents. However, it is often more effective to create local timelines of events in your ancestor's village. You can show the establishment of a new school, the day the railroad started operation, or the arrival and departure of the ministers at the local church.

TMG is easy to use and you may not need to refer to the user's manual for everyday operations. It does include a 229-page Reference Manual that is extensively indexed plus a separate 73-page Getting Started booklet. TMG also ships with a slide show demo disk that serves as an effective teaching tool: it shows TMG being put through its paces by an experienced user. This "learn by demonstrating" method is very effective at getting the new user up to speed quickly.

TMG uses a Menu Bar with pulldown menus in a manner similar to many computer programs. Most of the entries in the menus are intuitive and logical in sequence. Context-sensitive help is available at any time by pressing F1 or by selecting "Help" on the Menu Bar. The pulldown menus are supplemented by "hot keys" and "jump keys" that allow for quick navigation. Use of these special keys often allows for faster navigation than that of using the mouse. However, all these keys are optional. The new user will undoubtedly use the mouse for some time until the special keys become intuitive. Both methods work well.

Another feature that works well in TMG is that of "bookmarks." You may set a bookmark on a particular person and screen view; you can then quickly return to this same person and screen view at anytime with a few clicks of the mouse or a few keystrokes. For instance, you may find it helpful to set a bookmark for the father when working on a large family. You can then explore the children and their families, even the children's children and their spouses. However, you can quickly return to the original person's data entry screen at any time by using the "Return to Bookmark" function. A pop-up calendar is also provided with TMG along with a date calculator and a relationship calculator.

The default screen display is the Person View, a method of displaying all significant events recorded for one person's lifetime. The events are shown in chronological order which makes for an intuitive display. Unlike the simpler genealogy programs, TMG can show more than 32,000 different kinds of tags, most of them invented by the user. It can show such things as date entered the seminary, date and location graduated from the seminary, beginning and ending dates of military service (including multiple enlistments), dates of relocation of family, and so forth. As one person put it, "This program allows me to show information about my family such as dates and places when graduated, commissioned, canonized, or paroled."

The Family View screen is similar to a family group sheet, while the Tree View is more like the traditional pedigree chart. One nice feature of TMG is that when you exit the program it remembers the screen view and the person being viewed. Upon starting TMG the next time the same screen is loaded first, allowing you to begin where you left off.

TMG allows for up to one billion records in a database (assuming the hard drive is big enough to accommodate that) and multiple databases may be used. Data entry in TMG is simple and straightforward. All information is entered as a "tag" or a "flag." Tags can include such things as a name tag, a father/child relationship, a mother/child relationship, a birth event tag showing date and place, marriage event tag linking to a spouse, and so on. Flags are normally single-character items, such as gender (TMG allows three genders: male, female, and unknown), adopted, multi-birth, birthorder, and so on.

One of TMG's biggest appeals to the serious genealogist is its ability to record all data, even conflicting data. If you obtain information from three different sources about a person's date of birth, it's not unusual to find three different dates listed. Which one is correct? With simpler genealogy programs you need to guess at which is the most likely and then record that one date as "fact." You may find differing information years later that confirms or contradicts your earlier guess, you probably will no longer have the relevant details about each date available. However, with TMG you can record three (or more) dates of birth along with their sources and assign a surety level to each. If you later find a fourth source of the same information you can quickly check all three of the original dates and their sources in your database.

TMG also has the most flexible method of entering dates of any genealogy program. The following date formats can all be entered into the database at any time and reports will be displayed and sorted properly:

> 09/03/1845
>
> 1845.09.03
>
> 03/09/1845
>
> 03.09.1845
>
> 03-09-1845
>
> Sep 3, 1845
>
> SEP 3 1845
>
> 3 Sep 1845
>
> 3 SEP 1845
>
> after 1844
>
> between 1844 and 1846
>
> 1844 or 1845
>
> before 1846
>
> circa 1845
>
> 1845
>
> before Oct 1845
>
> after Aug 1845
>
> between Aug and Oct 1845
>
> 3 Sep or 4 Sep 1845

TMG has a built-in backup capability that makes backup copies of your database for archival and safety purposes. The default is that it automatically makes backups every time you exit the program, although you may turn this off if you wish. However, the backups are only written to another subdirectory on the same hard drive; it is up to the user to copy these backup files to floppy disks or tapes and to store them elsewhere for safekeeping. The backup files are "squeezed," a process that saves storage space.

Exhibits One of the most valuable objectives of genealogy research is to preserve evidence in a format that resembles the original as closely as possible. TMG provides Exhibits for this purpose. An exhibit may be a scanned photograph or a map, a sound file, or a text file that is a literal transcription of an original document. An Exhibit may be attached to any person, event, source, or repository. You can also have a "general exhibit" which is not attached to any record. The Exhibit Log is a filtered list of all the Exhibits contained within the database. This list can be examined in several different ways.

Research Log One item contained within TMG and not seen in many other genealogy programs is that of the Research Log. This is a database of the status of your research. It consists of tasks which you create and then update during the course of completing the tasks. It is essentially a list of items to be researched, not necessarily work already done. This is an excellent tool to use before traveling to a genealogy library or a courthouse to look at records. You can quickly see the tasks that you have planned to research there; some of these tasks may have been entered into the Research Log months or even years ago.

File Import TMG can import GEDCOM files created by any of the leading genealogy programs. In addition, it can directly read the databases of Roots III (a program produced by CommSoft, Inc.) and of Personal Ancestral File (an older genealogy program produced by the Mormons that was very popular).

~🖥~

Reports TMG has a heavy-duty reporting tool called the Custom Report Writer (CRW). CRW allows for the generation of thousands of different reports that can be printed on paper, displayed on screen, or written to a disk file. Even the program's GEDCOM file export routine was written in Custom Report Writer. The program ships with many standard reports already created for you but you can add many more to suit your needs. Once a new report format is created, it is automatically saved in the CRW Log so that you can generate similar reports again and again in the future.

The standard reports available in TMG are equal to those of any other high-end genealogy program. They include, in part:

- Ahnentafel report
- Descendancy report
- GEDCOM export
- Genealogy report
- "Linear ahnentafel" (straight line of descent from one ancestor to a selected individual)
- Many types of lists
- Pedigree chart
- An individual detail report (also known as the "Kitchen Sink Report") that prints everything about a person including name variations, all tags, and so forth
- Statistical report
- An audit of the database that is affectionately known as "The Sanity Checker" that looks for suspicious data (persons over 110 years old, individuals giving birth at very young ages, and so on)

Any of these reports can be modified as desired.

The Master Genealogist creates many reports that are for use with an external word processor, spreadsheet, or database program. You create these files in TMG, and then use your favorite word processor's features to enhance the reports and then to print them.

The Custom Report Writer, or CRW, allows for the creation of custom reports that the programmer never envisioned. For instance, if you want a report of all individuals in the database who are related to John Smith and who were born in Ireland and lived to be more than 80 years old, you can create such a report with the Custom Report Writer. The actual number of different reports that can be created is essentially infinite. However, CRW is one of the few features in THG that is not terribly intuitive or easy to use. Its power and many options require some thought, you probably will study the manual for a while before creating a custom report.

Using the Custom Report Writer, you can export a file to WordPerfect or Microsoft Word or any of more than 50 other word processing programs. The report may include footnotes, endnotes, a full index, table of contents, bibliography, special formatting, and so on. The end result is a high-quality genealogy book that does not resemble the "machine-generated" books produced by some of the earlier programs. Also, files that are lists of information can be exported in Lotus, Excel, dBase, or Multiplan formats, allowing for convenient exporting of data to other database or spreadsheet programs.

In summary, The Master Genealogist is an excellent program for use by either the genealogy newcomer or the experienced and demanding professional. The above description is a somewhat abbreviated list of some of the program's capabilities. A slide show demo of TMG is contained on the CD-ROM disc included with this book.

Roots IV This is the latest version of a very popular series of genealogy programs produced for years by CommSoft, Inc. The Roots series of programs have long had the reputation of being "the Cadillac of genealogy software." While today there are other programs competing for that title, Roots IV is still recognized as a "high-end program." CommSoft has promised that a Windows version will appear also.

Roots IV has many excellent features, probably the most notable one is its excellent printed reports. In fact, many genealogy books have been printed with Roots IV or its earlier Roots III version, no other word processor or desktop publishing program is required. Roots IV even has the capability to include pictures in its printed reports. However, for those who wish to add even more in the way of formatting or graphics, Roots IV will also export files in several popular word processing formats. With these files you can use your favorite word processing or desktop publishing program to add even more text formatting and graphics than is allowed in the stand-alone program.

Roots IV also has the highest learning curve of any of the genealogy programs available today. CommSoft includes a 499-page user's manual with Roots IV that does an excellent job of explaining the program's many features. The manual has many illustrations and many hints on how to use the program effectively. Most Roots IV users keep the manual in a convenient location and will refer to it frequently.

Roots IV is available in two versions: Standard and Extended. Both are the same price. The Standard Version of Roots IV requires at least a 286 AT-compatible computer with 640K of conventional memory plus at least another 2MB of expanded memory. The Extended Version of Roots IV requires at least a 386SX computer with 4MB of memory, although 8MB will result in much faster operation. Either extended or expanded memory will work. Performance on a 386SX computer will be leisurely, however. Most genealogists will want to use a higher-speed 386 or a 486 CPU for Roots IV. A minimum of 8MB of memory is required if you wish to use Roots IV in an MS-DOS window while running Microsoft Windows.

While Roots IV will work with a dot matrix printer, most genealogists will want to use a laser printer in order to take advantage of the rich variety of reports and the scanned graphics that are available. The program does not require a mouse, but again most users will probably want one in order to take advantage of its "shortcuts" to navigating around the program.

Both the Standard and the Extended versions require at least 20MB of disk space for the program and a database of 1,000 people. Larger databases will obviously require more space as Roots IV requires 2,500 bytes per individual in the database and more if text files are used. CommSoft suggests that Roots IV only be used on systems with at least 80MB hard drives. While a higher list price is usually mentioned, most dealers sell Roots IV at a discount price of $99.95.

~☐~

Most genealogy programs refer to "databases," with separate databases available for different genealogy projects. However, Roots IV refers to "projects." A study of a particular family may qualify as a "project." This terminology will appeal to professional genealogists who do research for hire for multiple clients; each client's work may be a separate project. Each project may contain nine million people in its database and essentially an infinite number of events and sources. The only real limitation is that of the disk space available.

Roots IV has a user interface that uses a combination of menus and "windows." These "windows" are not exactly the same as those of Microsoft Windows but do operate in a somewhat similar manner. It is possible to resize and reposition many of the windows, and multiple windows may be open at one time. The screen itself is referred to as "the desktop" and the various windows may be thought of as "documents" that are open on the desktop.

Data is entered in two different formats: structured data such as names, dates, and locations is entered in a "fill-in-the-blank" fashion, while text information is normally entered free form. Roots IV is also sometimes called a "linked database" in which certain fields in one document are logically connected to fields in a different document. For instance, a birth event is normally linked to the parents, and a birth date may be linked to a record of the source of that information. Frequently, multiple documents are linked to one source, such as a family Bible, that may contain birth and marriage information for many people. The information from the family Bible is entered once in one document, every person mentioned within that Bible has his or her record linked to that one source record.

Roots IV uses "Quick Entry Windows" for much of the data entry work. These windows are used to enter limited information for a person, a place, or a source. These windows make it easy to link new individuals, places, and sources not already in the computer's database.

Roots IV also has many other types of windows, and each may contain differing types of fields such as structured data fields, text fields, Check Boxes, Text Boxes, Restricted Windows, Unrestricted Windows, Text Windows with Push Buttons, List Windows, or Dialog Boxes. When multiple windows are open at once all this can be confusing. However, once accustomed to Roots IV's interface, you will find a place for every scrap of information that you care to collect.

The Menu Bar across the top of the screen is quite similar to many other programs and is easy to learn.

Fortunately, Roots IV has an excellent built-in Help System. Context-sensitive help is available at any point in the program by pressing F1 or by selecting Help on the Menu Bar. Also, a number of built-in online tutorials will lead the novice user through many of the more complex tasks in the program. Finally, tips are often displayed at the bottom of the screen when entering data or selecting new windows.

Types of Data Roots IV allows for the entry of almost any type of data that you obtain in your genealogy research. It also allows for conflicting data. For instance, you may obtain a person's date of birth from a census record, a different date of birth for the same person from a family Bible, and still a third date of birth from a pension application. In Roots IV you can create three or more birth events and record different dates in each. You can also assign different surety levels based upon your estimation of the accuracy of each. For instance, if the census record of 1850 listed the individual as a 3-year-old child, you would expect that record to be more accurate than a pension application made out 70 years later. (Yes, people lied about their ages years ago in the same manner as they do now.)

Dates Roots IV supports two types of dates: Free-form dates and Structured dates. A structured date is a traditional database field of day, month, and year. The Free-form date is a text field that holds up to 39 characters. You use this field when you wish to record data as it appeared in the original source. When you leave the Free-form date field the program attempts to interpret the free-form date and convert it to a structured date. A date that is written as "Jan. 13, 1845" will be converted to 1/13/1845. However, a date written as "January thirteenth 1843" will not. The free-form date is used on Genealogy Reports and other free-form text reports.

When using a structured date you can use a date modifier before the actual date. These modifiers are BEF (before), AFT (after), ABT (about), CA (circa or approximately), EST (estimated) or ??? (unknown).

Medical Data Roots IV keeps a medical database which can list the medical history of each individual. It can list height, weight, blood type, skin, eye color, hair color, and many medical conditions. These conditions include such things as allergies, arthritis, diabetes, epilepsy, scarlet fever, smallpox, and room for others in a field labeled "other."

Images Roots IV will accept images in three different formats: PCX (used by Zsoft and PC Paintbrush), GIF (CompuServe format), and TGA (Targa). External conversion utilities are available to convert a number of other formats to the three supported internally by Roots IV. Images may be displayed in two-color black and white, 16-colors, 256-colors, or 24-bit color depending upon any hardware limitations. These images may be pictures, drawings, or even maps. They can be displayed on screen and in many of the various reports.

Reports Probably the biggest strength of Roots IV is the wide variety of reports available. Also, Roots IV has among the best formatting capabilities available in a genealogy program. Many of the reports at the beginning of this chapter were produced with Roots IV. The reports available include the following:

Front Page—(prints a title page, credits or Table of Contents

Genealogy Format—prints Descendant, Ancestor, Family, and Generation reports in text format

Images—prints graphics files

Pedigree—prints 4, 5, or 6-generation Pedigree charts

Ahnentafel charts

Descendant—prints charts of descendants of a selected individual using text, direct drop, or indented formats

Relationship List—prints a report showing all the people related to a selected individual

Text—prints files not linked to a person or event, such as an introductory chapter in a family history book

End Notes—prints footnotes in a separate section

Index—Prints a back-of-the-book index of individuals, places, or marriages

Family Group Sheets Lists of many things can be printed, such as lists of individuals, events, marriages, mailing addresses or labels, roles, sources, and so on.

- ➲ Calendar
- ➲ Research Log
- ➲ Tiny Tafel

Most all of these reports can be printed directly to a printer or to a disk file to be used later.

Roots IV supports a new data exchange format called Event-Oriented GED-COM. This is a new enhancement to the GEDCOM standard that was invented by CommSoft. However, the new "standard" has not been adopted by any other genealogy programs so it is essentially useless today. Fortunately, Roots IV will also import and export regular GEDCOM files so data exchange may still be made with all the other genealogy programs.

In summary, Roots IV is a powerful and sophisticated genealogy program with a great deal of flexibility. It does an excellent job of recording all information in a genealogy research project. Roots IV has the widest variety of printed reports available in a genealogy program and will appeal to anyone whose primary interest is in printing a genealogy book. Its steep learning curve will be a problem to novices, but demanding genealogists will appreciate all the sophisticated capabilities available. A slide show demo of Roots IV is included on the CD-ROM disc that is included with this book.

Brothers Keeper (Shareware) Brothers Keeper is the leading shareware genealogy program. It may be deceptive at first: its user interface is so simple to use that you may not at first appreciate all the power and the capability of Brothers

Keeper. It has many different kinds of printed reports, some of which are not available in expensive commercial programs. Also, it supports scanned pictures and drawings in its database allowing you display ancestors' pictures on-screen.

As a shareware program, Brothers Keeper comes with the ultimate money back guarantee: If you don't like it you don't pay for it. Shareware programs may be used for evealuation for a limited period of time without payment. If you decide to keep the program and use it, you need to "register" the program by sending money to the author. In the case of Brothers Keeper, the registration fee is $45. After registering the program, you will receive a printed manual. You are also entitled to telephone and online support, and you will be notified of any new upgrades available.

You will need 512K or more of RAM memory in your computer to run Brothers Keeper, although the author recommends 640K bytes. While the program will operate directly from floppy disks, it is strongly recommended that you install the program and the data files on a hard disk because the program will run very slowly if the data is on a floppy disk.

Brothers Keeper has more printed reports available than any other shareware genealogy program. You will be able to print descendant charts that show how anyone in the file is related to everyone else. You also may print ancestor charts, family group sheets, alphabetical name lists, descendant trees, birthday and anniversary lists, ahnentafel charts, box charts, timelines, and customized reports. For each person entered you may include a date of birth, a date of death, and three other dates, and you may store a place of birth, a place of death, and a place for three other events. You may record source information for every date or location. You also may enter two additional fields that you may define. Each person may have up to seven message lines of additional data or a text file of unlimited size containing additional data. Fields are available to store the person's current mailing address. Each person may have up to eight marriages stored. Each marriage record can hold a marriage date, a place of marriage, one additional date and place, and divorce information, and each marriage can have 24 children.

Brothers Keeper (called BK for short) also fully supports the GEDCOM standard. It is common for someone to store a genealogy database in another program and then to use GEDCOM to import the data into BK whenever a fancy report is needed. Brothers Keeper can print the reports that may not be contained in other genealogy programs.

~🖥~

Brothers Keeper is menu-driven at all times. Its interface is slower than some programs but it is always easy to use. The main screen shows the following menu items:

Add names or link	Tree of descendants
Modify or look	anCestors
Individual add (single)	Group sheets
Edit text file	Register style report
Options	Box charts (descendants)
Help	4 family box charts
Descendants	3 more ancestor reports
ahnentafeL	merge 2 data files
Names-custom-birthday	split 1 database
Word search	gedcom import/eXport
Print strings	Utilities program
bacKup data files	* bar charts (statistics)
\ change directory	+ timeline chart
Stop	6 new reports

To select the routine you want to start, either type the letter that is capitalized (or the number) or use the arrow keys to select the desired routine and then press Enter. For instance, to display descendants you would press "D."

The screen used for most data entry is the Add screen which shows husband information in the top section of the screen, wife information below that, the marriage information next, and then child information. It is somewhat similar to a standard family group sheet. After each child is added, that child's information is erased from the screen and another child may be added. The way to add people is to first type in the husband, then the wife, then the marriage information, then each of their children in order of birth.

Dates are normally entered in the format of MMDDYYYY such as 09031845 for September 3, 1845. However, these dates may be displayed and printed by the program in any one of the following methods:

03-SEP-1845

03 SEP 1845

09/03/1845

09-03-1845

SEP-03-1845

SEP 03 1845

03-SEP-1845

03 SEP 1845

03-09-1845

1845.09.03

1845-09-03

If you prefer, you may specify that Brothers Keeper should never convert dates, it should always display them as entered. If so, a date entered as "September third, 1845" will be displayed in exactly the same manner. The downside of this is that the program is unable to sort by dates, so display of some information may occur in a nonchronological manner.

If you are not sure of a date, you may add additional information. The program will automatically recognize certain three-character abbreviations such as ABT for about, CIR for circa, BEF for before, and AFT for after. For example, if you know a person died before March 15, 1920, you may enter BEF 031520 and the program will convert it to BEF 15-MAR-1920. You may also enter dates with dual years such as 15-MAR-1680/81.

Brothers Keeper does have a file backup selection on the main menu; this allows for convenient copying of data files to a floppy disk.

Help Choosing H from the main menu will give you a brief summary of help information. Even though it is brief, it may remind you of what you need to know.

Also, at many times in the program the bottom line of the display will show you your choices as you are entering data and moving from field to field.

Printed Reports All print routines in Brothers Keeper may have the output sent to the PRINTER, to the SCREEN, or to a DISK file. There are two ways to write to a disk file. One way is to include the control codes (such as compressed and bold). This is useful if you want to print the information later. The other way is to send the output to a file without control codes. This method is useful if you wish to use a word processing or desktop publishing program to edit the file. When printing directly to paper most printers can be set up for different sizes of paper such as 8 ½ × 11 inches or A4 size paper.

Brothers Keeper has many reports available. Following is a list of some of them:

Descendants Report—will print the descendants of any one person. The descendant routine will show up to 30 generations.

Ahnentafel (Ahnentafel is from a German word meaning ancestor table)—this is a list of ancestors of a person, without drawing a chart like the Ancestor routine. You have the option to show relationships (such as parent, grandparent, and so on).

Name, Custom, Birthday—will print all names, birth dates, and code numbers in numerical order. If a name field is blank or is equal to "Not used" or is equal to "*UNKNOWN" or if a person has been deleted then it will not print.

Tree Print—will print a tree chart showing the descendants of any person with the parents and children connected with lines. The tree report will print up to 30 generations at a time.

Ancestor Charts—will print an ancestor chart for anyone in the file. The ancestor chart will show the person you choose and that person's parents, grandparents, great-grandparents, and so on. Birth, death, and marriage information also will print. You may choose eight different sizes of charts when printing. If you need to print more than seven generations, you will need to print multiple charts.

Group Sheets—will print the information for any person along with the person's parents, spouse, and children. Any message lines you entered may also be

printed with this routine if desired. The group sheets are useful if you are organizing your data, creating a book, or you wish to send the sheets to relatives for
further information.

Register Style Reports—will let you print register reports, indented reports, or
3 × 5 cards. The register and indented reports will print all the information
about all the descendants of a person and will optionally print an alphabetical index. If you intend to publish a book and use the register style report, you may
set the output to go to a disk file and then use your word processor or a desktop
publishing program to enhance the book. The register and indented reports will
give you several options for what information to include and how the report will
look. If you choose to have page numbers, it also will prepare for an alphabetical
index at the end. When the report is finished printing, you will have the option
to prepare an index file, and then sort the file.

Descendant Box Chart—will print a descendant chart that has each person in
a box and has lines connecting the boxes. The oldest person is at the top, the
person's children are below, and the grandchildren are below them, and so on.
Like most reports, the box charts may be printed, displayed, or sent to a disk
file. When you display the chart, you may use the arrow keys to move around
the chart. There is an option for small boxes with just dates, or larger boxes with
locations also. You may also adjust the width of the boxes. The width of the
boxes will affect the total number of people that can be printed in one generation and will also affect the length of the chart.

Four Family Box Chart—similar to the regular box chart described above, except it shows four families on the top line, and then all the descendants of those
four families with dotted lines connecting the four families where marriages occurred. When looking at a person in the third generation, it is a combination ancestor and descendant chart. The children that are common to more than one of
the families are only printed once under the first parent and a dotted line will
show the connection to the other parent's family.

Additional Ancestor Reports and Charts—can print multiple page ancestor reports, where the pages are cross referenced. You pick the starting person, and all
of the person's ancestors will be printed with four generations showing on each
page. You have the option to have each page start with the main person called
number 1 again, or to have the numbers continue to increase.

Ancestor Wall Chart—prints large charts with boxes for each person. This chart will contain nine generations (511 people) and will be about five feet high and two sheets of paper wide. It will include each person's name, the standard code number, and dates and locations for birth, marriage, death, and burial. People in the eighth and ninth generations will have abbreviated information.

Bar Charts—will be able to display and print statistics charts showing month of birth, month of marriage, month of death, number of children per marriage, and lifespan. You can, for example, print the lifespan of your ancestors.

Timeline Chart—will print or display the ancestors of a person showing the year of birth and death for each person. You can also include other events or other famous people on the chart by putting the information in the file BKEVENTS.TXT. The events in that file will print at the top of your chart, provided some of the ancestors that are printed also lived during that time period.

Direct Lineage Report—will show the connecting people between a person and one of his or her descendants. For example, you could pick your great grandfather and yourself and it would show your great grandfather and your great grandmother, your grandfather and grandmother, your father and mother, and you.

How Many Descendants a person has will tell you how many children, grandchildren, and so on. This is useful if you are going to print some other report for a person and want to know how big the report will be.

A Reasonableness Check of your database will find some common mistakes you can make when entering data. If you type in a date incorrectly such as 1990 instead of 1890, this report will catch it. You can set the limits for the ages, and it will print out the names of people who do not fall within the limits. If a birth date is blank for a person, it will not check that person's information for reasonableness. It will check the reasonableness of all people with standard dates.

Missing Information will show people that are missing birth dates, death dates, birth places, death places, or show people that do not have a father or mother.

List of All Surnames (Last Names) in the database will give you the number of people that have that name. After it compiles the list of names, you can print the list alphabetically, or you can print the list in order of popularity.

Listing of All Locations and What Events Happened at Those Locations—is useful if you are going to a certain county and want to know what documents to look for to verify the events that occurred in that area. You can either print all locations alphabetically with the events for each, or you can print only the locations that match the word or words you enter.

In summary, Brothers Keeper is a mature and complete genealogy program that is offered as shareware. It is easy to use and offers a wider variety of printed reports than any other shareware genealogy program. It is well supported by author John Steed both by telephone and online. Brothers Keeper will work on any PC, including the older XT clones. At a $45 registration fee, Brothers Keeper is an excellent choice.

A complete working copy of Brothers Keeper is included on the CD-ROM that accompanies this book.

Macintosh Genealogy Program

Reunion This is the most powerful Macintosh genealogy program available today. A product of Leister Productions, it includes all the features of Reunion for Windows detailed earlier. Leister Productions includes almost all the same features in both the Windows and the Macintosh versions of Reunion. The program includes full support of graphics and also multimedia support. It also closely integrates with your favorite Macintosh word processing program. Refer to the Reunion for Windows description earlier in this chapter, almost everything mentioned there applies equally to the Macintosh version.

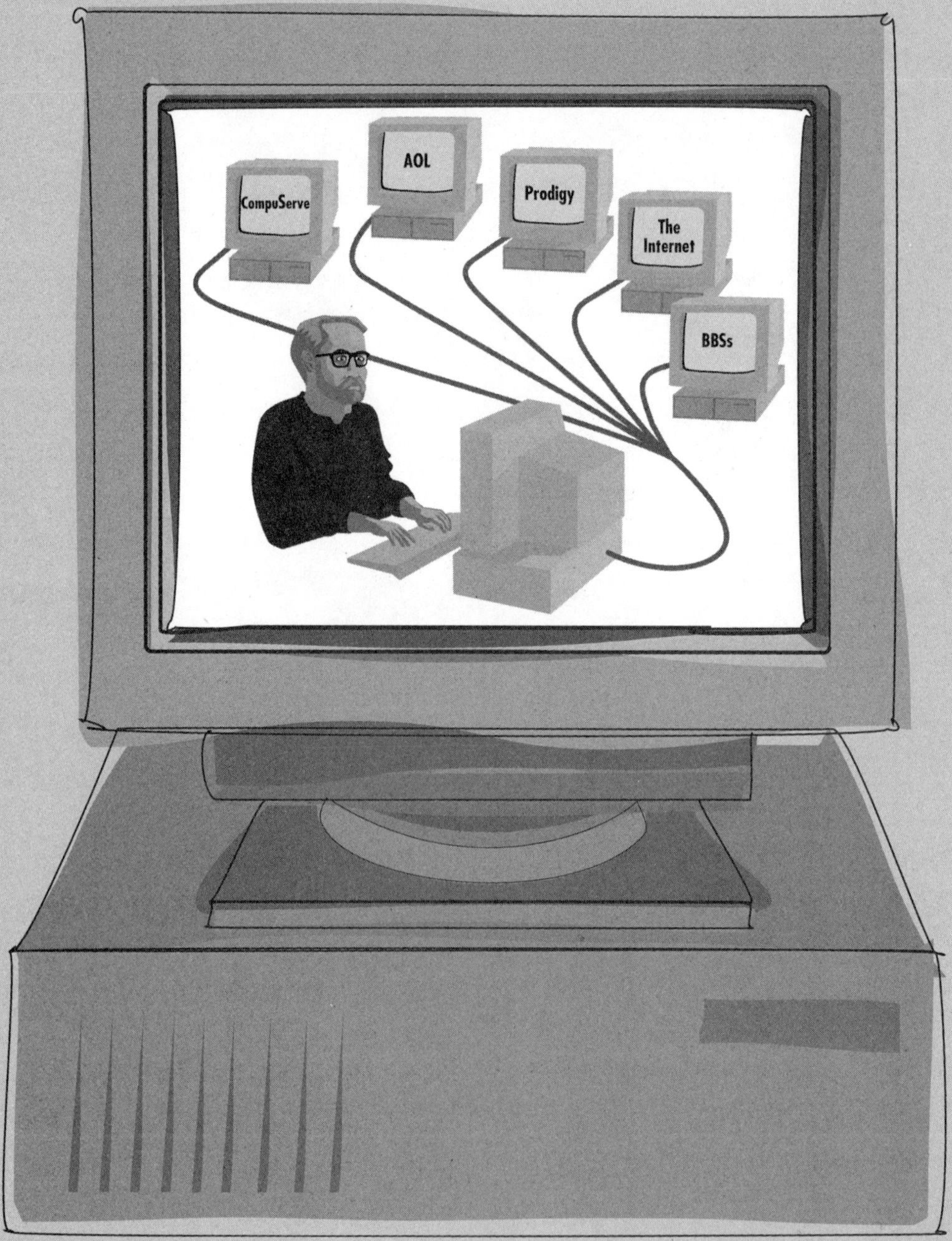
CompuServe
AOL
Prodigy
The Internet
BBSs

4 | *Online Sources and Assistance*

The
biggest change in genealogy in the past decade has been the growth in available genealogy assistance from online data services. With the use of a home computer equipped with a modem, the genealogist can now compare notes with thousands of other genealogists around the world quickly and easily without ever leaving home. Some genealogy records are available to you, and online databases of Social Security death records can also be accessed. There's a wealth of genealogy software and utilities that can be retrieved over the telephone lines and then stored on your hard drive or floppy disks. You can do this by joining in the genealogy groups that exist on all the major online services. These "electronic genealogy clubs" are available 24 hours a day, 7 days a week. The information available varies widely as does the ease of use. We will examine the five most popular sources of online genealogy assistance:

1. CompuServe's Genealogy Forums
2. Prodigy's Genealogy Bulletin Board
3. America Online's Genealogy Club
4. Internet's varied genealogy groups
5. Bulletin Board Systems, including FidoNet's Genealogy "echoes"

These five groups are all available via modem from your home computer. The first three are commercial services that run on mainframe computers and are organized and managed by those services. The Internet groups and bulletin board systems are "distributed services" with information and messages loosely organized.

CompuServe

As the oldest and the largest of all the online services, CompuServe has much to offer the genealogist. It is the most mature of all the online services and has by far the most content available. Not only does it have two online sections or "forums" devoted to genealogy, it also has other databases of interest to many genealogists. These include an up-to-date online database of telephone listings, a database of voter registrations, and the Social Security Administration's death records. These databases are not available on the other online services.

CompuServe has news, weather, and sports information from a number of on-line news services along with a wide variety of financial information. Com-puServe's "roots" are in the financial information services arena where the company first attained prominence. It has more than 700 discussion forums— far more than any of the other commercial services. It is the primary source of computer support; more than 900 hardware and software companies provide di-rect support to their customers via CompuServe. In the 15 or so years that it has been in the online business, CompuServe has grown to more than 2,700 differ-ent online services now serving more than 3 million active members. It is a wholly-owned division of H&R Block, Inc.

CompuServe's electronic mail offerings are the most full-featured of all the on-line services. You can send electronic mail to 13 different mail systems, includ-ing the Internet, MCI Mail, AT&T Mail, cc:Mail, and MHS (a popular messaging system on local area networks). You can even send a fax.

CompuServe's base prices are generally higher than its competitors, although experienced users know how to minimize their monthly charges through the use of "automated communications programs" that will be discussed later. Use of these specialized programs often results in lower prices than for doing the same tasks on CompuServe's competitors. There are two pricing plans available.

The plan that is the most popular is the "Standard Pricing Plan" at $9.95 per month. The Standard Pricing Plan includes unlimited online time for more than 100 different services. It also includes 3 hours per month of online time con-nected to the Internet. The Standard Pricing Plan also allows you to send approx-imately 270 pages of full-text electronic mail messages per month. The exact number of messages will depend upon how much text is in each one, but most members report being able to send 100 to 200 messages per month without in-curring any extra fees. For all services not included in the Standard Pricing Plan's 100 unlimited time services, the online charge is $4.80 per hour at modem speeds of 300 baud through 28,800 baud. These rates are in effect 24 hours a day, 7 days a week. There is no surcharge for using CompuServe during business hours.

In addition, CompuServe has a special plan for those who use the Internet access a lot. This plan allows access for as little as 75 cents per hour with a minimum charge of $15 per month.

Among the services that are bundled in with unlimited usage in the Standard Pricing Plan are the following:

Accu-Weather Maps/Reports

Associated Press Online

National Weather Service

Online Today Daily Edition

Reuters Canadian News Clips

Reuters UK News Clips

Reuters/Variety Entertainment

Consumer/Finance Columns

Entertainment Columns

Roger Ebert

Lifestyles Columns

Opinion/Commentary Columns

American Heritage Dictionary

Consumer Reports

Consumer Reports Complete Drug Reference

Grolier's Academic American Encyclopedia

HealthNet

Information Please Business Almanac

Information Please General Almanac

Peterson's College Database

Online Inquiry

Basic Current Stock Quotes

FundWatch Online By Money Magazine

Hollywood Hotline™

People Magazine Daily Edition

Roger Ebert's Movie Reviews

Soap Opera Summaries

Classified Ads

CompuServe Mail

EAASY SABRE Airline Reservations

WORLDSPAN Travelshopper Airline Reservations

Bed & Breakfast Database

MAGELLAN Basic Maps

Zagat Restaurant Survey

The above list is abbreviated, you can obtain a full list online. Note too that unlike other online services, you have unlimited time on the above sections of CompuServe. You are not limited to 5 hours of free time per month in these sections. This makes CompuServe very popular for professionals who have automated "scripted programs" to connect every hour or so and quickly grab the latest stock quotes or the latest news. These programs can run automatically with no human intervention required.

The two genealogy forums on CompuServe are not bundled in the above unlimited usage services, they are charged at $4.80 per hour for online time. The same is true for most of the 2,600 services not shown in the above list.

The "Alternative Pricing Plan" is most popular among business users who only use CompuServe for electronic mail (e-mail) and perhaps for financial services. The basic monthly fee is $2.50 and then the CompuServe member pays for all online time by the minute. Online rates are $6.00 to $18.00 per hour depending upon baud rate. Anyone who is interested in using the genealogy services on CompuServe will probably prefer the Standard Pricing Plan instead.

CompuServe has its own worldwide network with more than 40,000 public dial-up ports around the world. There are local access numbers available in most parts of the United States as well as in major cities throughout Canada, Europe, and the Pacific Rim countries. CompuServe has local direct numbers available in such places as Bangkok, Thailand, and Christchurch, New Zealand. When dialing any of these direct CompuServe numbers there is no surcharge for international communications. CompuServe now has 14,400 baud connections available in most areas throughout North America and in major European cities and Pacific Rim countries as well. They are also presently converting their network to 28,800 baud connections. Busy signals are rarely encountered when dialing into CompuServe's network.

In addition to their own network, you can access CompuServe via many other data networks throughout the world. CompuServe can be reached via local telephone numbers in more than 100 countries, although communications surcharges are normally imposed by these other networks. Also, if you have local access to the Internet you can connect directly to CompuServe via an Internet Telnet session. CompuServe has several hundred thousand members outside of North America.

CompuServe members are assigned a "User ID" that is all numeric with one comma. For instance, 76701,263 is a typical CompuServe User ID. This number is the "electronic address" of the member although full names are normally shown as well. Most CompuServe members do use their full names online also although it is not a strict requirement to do so. The use of "handles" or "screen names" is discouraged in most areas of CompuServe, although they may be common on some of the electronic games and other services.

If you need assistance with the use of Compuserve, you can call their Customer Service department at 1-800-848-8990. If you are online, you can obtain Customer Service assistance by typing GO FEEDBACK which takes you to an area of CompuServe that is free of online charges. If your questions are specific to genealogy or to the topics of any of the other hundreds of forums, you can go to the appropriate forum and enter a message addressed "To: SYSOP" and normally you will receive an answer from an expert there within a few hours.

Connecting to CompuServe can be very simple. Unlike most other online services, you do not need any special communications software to connect to CompuServe. Almost all of the "terminal emulator" programs will work. However, if you obtain one of the programs designed for exclusive use with CompuServe you will find the service to be much easier to use and your online time and charges will be reduced significantly. Most CompuServe members use one of the specialized programs.

CompuServe itself produces communications programs for Windows, MS-DOS, OS/2, and Macintosh. It is not necessary to own a Macintosh or a PC; owners of Amiga, Atari, UNIX, and other computer systems may also access CompuServe's services. A special version of one of CompuServe's Windows programs can be found on the CD-ROM disc in the front of this book. You can install CompuServe's software and be online within a very few minutes. The programs provided by CompuServe are very user-friendly and graphical; navigating around the service is quickly learned. Also, there are free areas on the service where the newcomer may spend some time learning the basics of using CompuServe effectively.

CompuServe's greatest strength may also be one of its drawbacks: The service may be customized in myriad ways. Unlike most other online services, you have a variety of "front-end communications programs" to choose from. CompuServe does supply software for use in MS-DOS, Windows (two different programs), OS/2, and Macintosh (two different programs), but third-party vendors also offer more than a dozen other communications programs that will entirely replace CompuServe's software in your computer. Many of these programs add extra functions not offered in the programs supplied by CompuServe. Many of them are "automated communications programs" that can cut your online time and charges in half or even more.

Automated communications programs operate under the philosophy that a computer can always enter commands faster and more efficiently than a human being. Almost all of these automated programs operate so that a human never

CompuServe opening screen

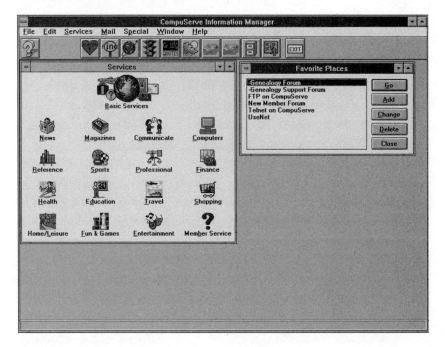

touches the keyboard while the computer is communicating with CompuServe.
These programs allow you to tell your computer what functions are to be done
before the connection to CompuServe is made. The computer then dials under
program control, executes whatever instructions you have specified, stores the information on the local disk drive, and then logs off. All the requested information (messages, files, mail, stock quotes, weather maps, and so on) may be read
at your leisure after disconnecting from CompuServe and while you are not in-
curring online charges. Since you are charged only for online time, anything that
reduces that time will save money.

Most of these automated communications programs also include mini word
processors that you use for composing new mail or new forum messages. A few
even include spell checkers. Again, you compose all messages offline at your

leisure when you are not paying for the online time. You may stop and look up information as you wish. You may compose any number of messages offline.

Once all offline operations are completed, the automated communications program dials back to CompuServe, sends all the new information at maximum modem speed, and then disconnects. When using only one or two forums and also using a high-speed modem, it is common for online sessions to be only 1 or 2 minutes. You pay only for the actual time spent online.

Many of these programs add other useful functions, such as automated address books of User IDs, long-term storage of captured messages and files that have been downloaded, online help information, and so on.

Other third-party programs allow for frequent automated checks of stock market prices or for following certain news or sports stories. Many of these will log on and capture the needed information while the computer is unattended. For instance, you can program one of these third-party packages to log on and capture the latest stock market quotes on selected stocks every hour and then dial a pocket pager if the price on any stock goes above or below preselected thresholds.

All of the automated communications programs will still allow you to access the same data as you would with any of CompuServe's interactive programs. However, the on-screen displays may look different.

The figure on the next page shows a message on CompuServe's Genealogy Forum as displayed in CompuServe Information Manager for Windows. The figure on page 85 shows the same message displayed in OzCIS for Windows, a popular automated communications program.

Deciding which automated communications program is best for you can be difficult. While most of these add extra functions and can also reduce online time and charges, some of them are more complex to set up and use. Following is a partial list of the available front-end communications programs.

Navigator for Windows is a program available directly from CompuServe. It may be ordered by mail, it may be stocked in most larger computer stores, or it can be ordered while online with a different communications program. You can

Sample Information Manager screen

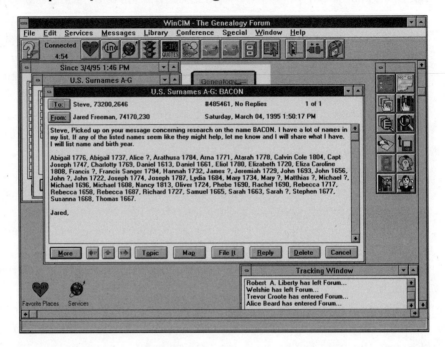

type GO WINNAV for all the details. The price is $30, but it comes with a usage credit that will offset much if not all of that price.

OzCIS for Windows is a $60 shareware program that has become very popular. It is based on the popular MS-DOS program called OzCIS. The author has added much more capability and, of course, full use of the Windows interface. OzCIS for Windows has a built-in spell checker that can be used when composing new messages offline. OzCIS has a more difficult learning curve than some of the other programs, but it also has more capabilities than most.

NavCIS for Windows is a program available in both a limited free version and in a commercial version. The free version is an excellent program by itself, but upgrading to the commercial version adds extra functions. Full details are available online on CompuServe by typing GO DVORAK. The cost varies between free for the limited edition to $99 for the full version.

→ ## Sample OzCIS screen

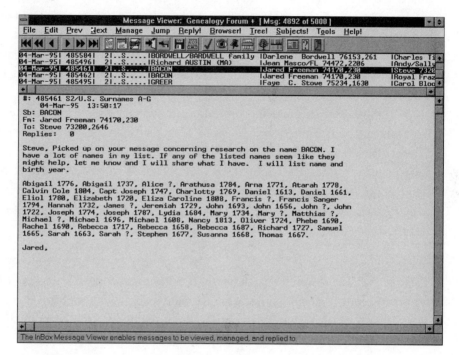

TAPCIS is a $79 DOS shareware "front-end communications program" for CompuServe that has been very popular for years. It has many extra add-on utilities available both from the producers as well as from others. While newer and flashier programs have come along since, TAPCIS remains the venerable workhorse for many thousands of satisfied users. It runs quickly in 640K of memory and works well even in palmtops with limited storage capacity. TAPCIS may be downloaded online by typing GO TAPCIS.

OzCIS is the MS-DOS version of the OzCIS for Windows program listed previously and has similar features. The MS-DOS version is a $40 shareware program. It requires an 80286 or better computer with at least 2MB of memory available. OzCIS has a built-in spell checker that can be used when composing new messages offline.

NavCIS for MS-DOS is a program that is very similar to the Windows version listed previously, with the same price range.

AutoSig is best known for its price: It's free. It is one of the oldest of the "automated front-end communications programs" but does have the drawback of being harder to set up and make operational. It's recommended for the experienced CompuServe users only and can be downloaded online by typing GO PCCOM.

ACCIS is a $69 commercial communications program that squeezes many functions into very limited storage space. It is designed especially for use on Hewlett-Packard and other palmtop computers. You can travel the world and keep your CompuServe computer in a coat pocket. It will also work well on any desktop PC, requiring you to learn only one program for use in both environments. You can obtain more information about ACCIS online by typing GO HPHAND.

There is only one CompuServe automated communications program available for the Macintosh. The good news is that many people with multiple computers report that Navigator is one of the finest, if not the finest, such program available. **CompuServe Navigator for Macintosh** can be purchased in many computer stores or ordered online on CompuServe by typing GO NAVIGATOR. Its retail price is $79.95 and includes credits for online time.

There are other automated communications programs available for Amiga, Atari, UNIX, CP/M, Apple II, and many other computer systems as well.

In most cases, it is best to first use CompuServe's own program: CompuServe Information Manager. It is available in four versions: MS-DOS, Windows, OS/2, and Macintosh. The Windows version is included on the CD-ROM disc in the front of this book. Also, IBM includes a copy of the OS/2 version of CompuServe Information Manager in every copy of OS/2 that it ships. The MS-DOS and Macintosh versions may be purchased at most computer stores and at most large bookstores for about $25. You may also order them online from CompuServe if you have logged on with a different program. Once accustomed to CompuServe you may find that you want to move up to one of the more powerful front-end communications programs.

CompuServe has begun to move away from the role of "an online service" to become that of an "information provider." The information may still be online or it may be CD-ROM–based.-CompuServe now produces bimonthly CD-ROM discs that are somewhat like "electronic magazines" featuring current information about services available. Each of these discs is full multimedia with sound clips, graphics files, and even full-motion video. Also an updated database of many of the files available for downloading is on each disc. You can search that database on the CD-ROM disc and decide which files you wish to obtain, if any. Your computer will later dial out and retrieve those files without any further human interaction required.

Each of the CD-ROM discs also contains three copies of CompuServe Information Manager for Windows; one each in English, French, and German. At the time of this writing, the only CompuServe CD-ROMs available are for Windows but a Macintosh version is in the works.

The Genealogy offerings on CompuServe are available in three places:

The **Genealogy Forum** is the established place for genealogy assistance.

The **Genealogy Vendor Support Forum** is a new service that is devoted to the support of services of several organizations in the genealogy business. You can go to the Genealogy Vendor Support Forum to receive technical support directly from employees of these businesses as well as to compare notes with others who use these services.

CompuServe's Internet Gateway is the third area of interest to genealogists. The Internet now has newsgroups of interest to genealogists and some files that may be downloaded (retrieved) that contain some genealogy information. CompuServe's Internet services include full access to World Wide Web, gopher, ftp files, Telnet access to other computers and access to Usenet news groups. CompuServe's Internet gateways allow easy access to many of Internet's more cryptic commands and can simplify the use of Internet services. CompuServe is the only major online service to offer PPP (Point-To-Point Protocol) access for the Internet, a particularly attractive feature for anyone using any of the more sophisticated

Internet access programs. Also, CompuServe has the lowest online charges for World Wide Web access of all the major online systems.

The **Genealogy Forum** is the largest and busiest area on CompuServe for genealogists. Any member can visit by use of CompuServe's "GO Words," in this case it's GO ROOTS.

➡ **CompuServe's Genealogy Forum welcome screen**

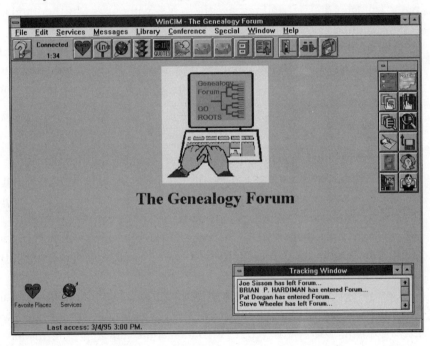

There are four sysops (system operators) on the Genealogy Forum to help you, including the author of this book. The other sysops are Gay Spencer, Phil DeSilva, and Michael Mac Cannell; all are experienced genealogists. Also, a Genealogy Book Review Editor, Martha Reamy, and an Adoption Search Specialist, Vikki Schummer, are on the online staff. These two are recognized experts at their specialties. None of these staff members are CompuServe employees, they all access the network from their homes to help others on the forum. A number of professional genealogists are members of the forum also. However, the vast majority of members range between genealogy newcomers to experienced amateurs.

CompuServe's Genealogy Forum is divided into four primary functions:

- Message Board
- File Libraries
- Member Directory
- Online conferences

Message Board   The Genealogy Forum's message board is the busiest part of the genealogy services on CompuServe. More than 1,000 messages may be posted in a single day covering a wide variety of topics. If you are not using one of the automated communications programs mentioned earlier it is best to keep a log file open or use some other method of writing the many messages to your local disk drive. You can then spend time reading messages later while offline. You might want to look up information before replying to a message, this is simplified if the messages are stored on your disk drive.

One of the nice features of CompuServe's forum message boards is that a message may either be addressed to a specific individual or broadcast as a message to everyone. If you are involved in sending and receiving messages on the Genealogy Forum, you are automatically notified of any new messages addressed to you as soon as you enter the forum. You then can use a GET WAITING MESSAGES command and read the ones addressed to you.

The Genealogy Forum's message board is divided into 18 sections:

I "I'm new and..."

2 U.S. Surnames A-G

3 U.S. Surnames H-M

4 U.S. Surnames N-S

5 U.S. Surnames T-Z

6 Canadian Genealogy

7 UK&Irish Genealogy

8 European Genealogy

9 Latin America

10 All other countries

11 Jewish Genealogy

12 Societies/Libraries

13 How to find records

14 Software/Computers

15 History/Heraldry

16 Adoption Searches

17 Wandering messages

18 Ask the SYSOPs

Technical help with genealogy software is always available. The figure on the next page shows a typical help screen.

File Libraries   A major advantage of CompuServe's Genealogy Forum is the huge number of files available for downloading to your computer. The Genealogy Forum on CompuServe is the largest repository of genealogy-related files available anyplace online. You are able to transfer these files across the telephone lines to your computer and store them on your disk drive. These files then may be used time and time again without connecting online.

There are more than 7,000 genealogy-related files including all the shareware genealogy programs available for Windows, MS-DOS, Macintosh, Amiga, and so on. Even genealogy programs for older computers such as CP/M and TRS-80 are available for downloading. All binary files on CompuServe's Genealogy Forum are checked for viruses before being made available to everyone.

WinCIM help screen

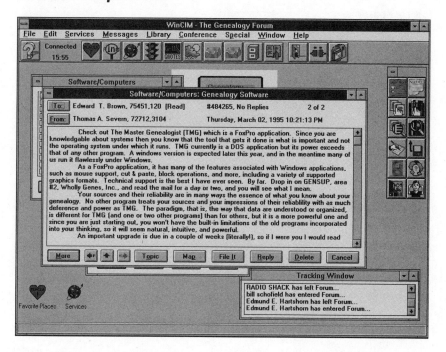

There are numerous text files geared to the newcomer on a wide variety of topics. The Family History Library in Salt Lake City also maintains most of their informational brochures online in the file libraries.

The File Libraries are divided into 15 sections:

1 New to Genealogy?

2 Windows Software

3 MS-DOS Software

4 Macintosh Software

5 Other Software

6 Text Files

7 Information about Surnames

8 Tiny Tafel files

9 Societies & Organizations

10 Salt Lake City records

11 Public Archives

12 Book Reviews

13 Genealogy Magazines

14 Graphics Files

15 CompuServe Information

The "New to Genealogy?" section contains many text files designed to help the newcomer learn how to do genealogy, and several files explaining different facets of genealogy. Among some of the most popular files found here are:

➡ **ROOTS.MAP—Users' Guide to the Genealogy Forum** Revision #11 of a users' guide to the Genealogy Forum. This ASCII text file describes how the Genealogy Forum is organized and what services are available. Users of CompuServe Information Manager (CIM) will find this guide especially valuable.

➡ **COUSIN.TXT—How to Calculate Cousin Relationships** Have you ever wondered what "third cousin, twice removed" means? This text file contains a chart that explains it all.

➡ **QUICK.TIP—Sandy Clunies' Hints on Starting a Genealogy Search** "Quick Tips for the New Family Researcher—From A to Z." This is a brief ASCII text file prepared by Sandy Clunies in response to a request. It lists a lot of information and hints for the newcomer to genealogy. (Oldtimers are encouraged to read it as well!) This is probably the best collection of hints and "how to's" available in less than 9,000 bytes. Keep this on your hard disk and refer to it often.

➡ **GENBOO.EXE—Genealogy Source Book & Self-Help Guide**   This is a self-expanding PC-compatible Microsoft Word for Windows V 6.0 file. It is a compilation of the main self-help guides found in the "New to Genealogy" section of the Genealogy Forum. Organized and complete with a table of contents and all references. Uploaded by Ron Collins.

➡ **INQLTR.ZIP—Inquiry Letter Examples**   One rewarding way to further your research is to write to "blind leads"—especially modern-day descendants of elusive ancestors, like those found via a Phone*File search. This file gives you good tips on how to write letters that get answered; two example letters are included for your use.

The four software sections of the Libraries contain a large amount of genealogy software. Almost every shareware and free genealogy program or utility program of interest to genealogists will be found there.

The Tiny Tafel Files Library contains thousands of such files; they are collected and compressed into "collections" frequently. You can quickly download these compressed files and then use the Tiny Tafel Editor program by Christopher Long (available in the MS-DOS Software Library) to quickly compare your Tiny Tafel file against those of thousands of other CompuServe members.

The Societies and Organizations Library contains a database of more than 4,000 groups around North America along with detailed information on many of them. Lists of major libraries and collections of genealogy archives are also listed there.

The Family History Library in Salt Lake City provides many services and publications about how to conduct research. While you can obtain these publications by writing to the Library, you can also download them from the "Salt Lake City records" Library on the Genealogy Forum.

One section that is unique to CompuServe is the Genealogy Book Reviews section which functions as an online database of thousands of genealogy book reviews. Each is reviewed by Martha Reamy, an avid book reviewer and former genealogy magazine editor.

The Genealogy Magazines Library is one of the newer services on the forum, it includes complete tables of content from hundreds of genealogy publications.

If you find a topic that looks interesting you then contact the publishers directly to order back copies.

The Graphics Files Library contains many scanned photos of historical interest along with numerous other pictures. Many members have uploaded pictures of coats of arms to this library; these can make interesting Windows wallpaper. The same is true for photos of Scottish tartans for several clans that are available for downloading.

Searching for a file is rather easy as the software is "point and click" in CompuServe Information Manager.

The figure on the next page shows the file FT4WIN.ZIP, a popular shareware genealogy program. You can quickly see the file name and its size of 726,146 bytes, which means that it can be downloaded in about 8 minutes at 14,400 baud. The file has previously been downloaded 2,521 times by other Genealogy Forum members. The User ID of the person who placed it on CompuServe's Genealogy Forum is 70152,1355 (who is the author of the program).

One of the advantages of downloading files from CompuServe is the use of their "B" protocol. If the file transfer gets interrupted before completion, the partial file can be stored on your disk drive. You can then connect later and go back and download only the remainder of the file, it is not necessary to start from the beginning again. This can be very useful when plagued with noisy telephone connections.

Member Directory   The Member Directory is a database internal to the Genealogy Forum that lists "who is interested in which surnames." You can enter this database and quickly find out who else has previously expressed an interest in the surnames that you are interested in. You then can send a message to those members in order to compare notes. While in the Member Directory you will want to enter your genealogy interests so that others may find you in the future.

The figure on page 96 shows an example of a search for anyone interested in the name **Eastman**. In this case, the window on the left shows all the Genealogy Forum members who have previously registered an interest in the surname Eastman. Moving the mouse and double-clicking on any one person's name, such as Gay Spencer, pops up the second window showing the details on that person's entry in the database. In this case you can see all her surname interests listed, including Eastman. You also see her electronic address of 76702,1353 so that

Genealogy shareware program

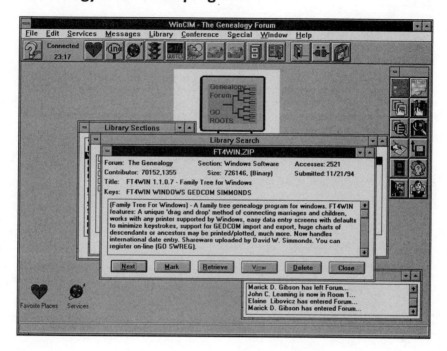

you may send a message to her on the Genealogy Forum or via CompuServe Mail.

Online Conferences   An online conference is an opportunity to "converse" with other CompuServe members live, keyboard-to-keyboard. On the Genealogy Forum there is a standing conference that starts every Tuesday night at 10:00 p.m. eastern standard time that is an "open topic" discussion group. These conferences are very popular, often attracting 40 people or more at a time. It can be a very fast-paced environment with many people online at once, multiple conversations go flashing by your screen interwoven in a manner that takes some getting used to.

On other evenings there may be specialized topic conferences. These may be devoted to things such as Southern genealogy research, Black American research,

Surname search

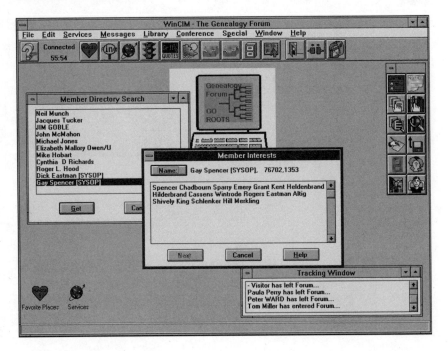

Hispanic genealogy, Acadian research (in both Louisiana and Eastern Canada), and Photographing Tombstones. Many of these specialized topics will have a moderator who functions as a coordinator for the topic that evening. The topics of these conferences change constantly; check the online announcements to see what is presently scheduled.

The conference rooms are actually available all the time. Frequently, members will drop into a conference area just to see who is there and to take part in genealogy conversations. You may see these unscheduled conferences happening at almost any hour of the day.

The Genealogy Forum has three conference rooms so that up to three conversations may take place simultaneously.

The Genealogy Vendor Support Forum   CompuServe recently opened a second "forum" for genealogists. It is a "vendors support forum" providing online services to cusomers and members of several leading providers of genealogy services. Each of these vendors has employees available daily to answer questions, offer assistance, and provide various tips. Also the file libraries on this forum have many text files and programs devoted to the services of these vendors. Presently there are six organizations represented and more are expected.

The six sections of the forum are

1. New England Historic Genealogical Society, the largest genealogy society in the United States. The Society keeps many of its catalogs and brochures available online, and an employee of the Society is available daily to answer questions.

2. Wholly Genes Software, producers of "The Master Genealogist" software for MS-DOS. A demo version of the program is available for downloading as are numerous technical text files. Also, the Library contains a collection of "timelines" submitted by users of The Master Genealogist.

3. Leister Productions, producers of "Reunion" software for Windows and Macintosh. Demo versions of the programs and users' groups newsletters are available for downloading.

4. Brothers Keeper, the most popular MS-DOS shareware genealogy program available today. The entire program and several additional utility programs may be downloaded from the Brothers Keeper Library.

5. CommSoft, Inc., producers of "Roots IV" software for MS-DOS. CommSoft has a demo version of Roots IV available for downloading, plus their popular RUG (Roots Users' Group) newsletter and a variety of other technical notes.

6. The Family Edge, a popular genealogy program available in both shareware and commercial versions for MS-DOS. The complete shareware version is available in The Family Edge Library.

Each of the above vendors has their own message board section, their own File Library section, and an online conference room for live chats. The files in the Libraries are generally a mixture of items supplied by these organizations and by their members and customers. In the case of the New England Historic Genealogical Society, many text files are available that describe their many activities and services. The software companies' File Libraries generally provide technical information, users' groups information, updated software releases, and third-party add-on utilities.

CompuServe's Internet Gateway   All CompuServe members have access to all the genealogy information on the Internet services, including World Wide Web, Telnet, ftp, and Usenet Newsgroups. CompuServe members have the option of connecting through terminal emulation or by PPP (Point-to-Point Protocol), and it is the only one of the commercial online services to offer that choice.

All CompuServe members get 3 hours of Internet usage per month as part of the regular membership fee. For high-volume Internet users, CompuServe has the Internet Club, which offers 20 hours of access to Internet services for a $15 monthly fee (in addition to the basic $9.95 monthly membership fee). Additional Internet hours will be billed to club members at $1.95 per hour. CompuServe also supplies free copies of Mosaic software for use with World Wide Web.

The information available through CompuServe's Internet gateways will be same as that available through other Internet connections. This will all be discussed at some length in the section of this book devoted to the Internet.

Phone*File   One of the most interesting ways to find distant relatives is by searching telephone directories all over the country. Indeed, several companies have marketed "books" containing listings of individuals with a certain surname and have occasionally even hinted that these were "genealogy books." This method of seeking others with the same surname can be especially effective when looking for a long-lost relative, an unknown relative in a divorce case, or even just finding out who else in the country might be descended from that immigrant great-grandparent with the unusual last name.

It isn't practical to search large numbers of telephone books on paper or microfiche. There are telephone directories published on CD-ROM discs. However, these CD-ROM discs are expensive for casual use and they quickly become outdated.

CompuServe has a service called Phone*File that provides over 80 million U.S. residential telephone listings, complete with addresses. The information on Phone*File is updated monthly.

Phone*File applies a surcharge of 25 cents per minute but you can usually find the information you want within 10 or 15 minutes for less-common surnames. If you are going to use telephone directories only occasionally or you want the very latest listings, the Phone*File service on CompuServe is probably the most cost-effective method of obtaining the information. If you are going to do a lot of telephone database searches, then paying between $50 to $200 for a CD-ROM database may be the better choice.

Script files or programs that automate the process of searching all 50 states and the District of Columbia have become popular for use with Phone*File. Using one of these scripts speeds up the process tremendously, saving you money in online charges.

COMPUTRACE   Another service available online is COMPUTRACE. This database will allow you to research recent and historical city, state, and zip code of residence for over 100 million U.S. citizens, both living and deceased. COMPUTRACE actually consists of two different databases:

The COMPUTRACE Living File, which contains information on 60 million individuals whose names appear in public record filings in 27 states.

The COMPUTRACE Deceased File, which contains information on over 40 million individuals whose death occurred after 1928. All individuals contained within this file were United States citizens residing anywhere in the U.S. or in one of 14 other countries at the time the individual's death was reported. This information was obtained from the Social Security death records, including year of birth, partial Social Security number, the state that issued the Social Security number, the year the Social Security number was issued, the date of death, and the zip code of the recipient of the subject's lump sum death benefit (if applicable).

In short, the wide variety of services available to genealogists makes Compu-Serve a very attractive service.

Prodigy

Another major online system of interest to genealogists is Prodigy, a joint venture between IBM and Sears. Prodigy has been heavily marketed and the name is familiar to most computer owners. Prodigy's on-screen navigation system is easy to use, making it a good choice for anyone new to computers, especially children. Prodigy has more sections for children than any of the other online systems.

 Prodigy opening screen

Prodigy also has very aggressive pricing. The base rate is $9.95 per month which includes 5 hours of online time. Additional time is billed at $2.95 per hour. Also, Prodigy offers a "Value Plan" that is $14.95 per month with unlimited time on certain core services (not the Genealogy Bulletin Board, however). The Value Plan also includes 5 hours of the "plus services" and then bills at $2.95 an hour for anything over 5 hours in those services.

Prodigy also offers a wide variety of news, weather, and sports information. This system uses computer graphics heavily, making it easy to find the news articles you want by clicking with the mouse on colorful icons. Stock market quotes are also available. Unlike some of the other services, there is no method to obtain this information automatically with "script files," you must sit in front of the computer and use the mouse in an interactive method. Prodigy offers e-mail to anyone with an Internet address. You can also send faxes from Prodigy.

Prodigy is limited to users of MS-DOS, Windows, or Macintosh operating systems. You must use Prodigy's own proprietary software. There is very little communications software available from third-party programmers and there is no method of accessing Prodigy in terminal emulation mode.

Prodigy's menu system is easy to use and the newcomer will quickly learn to navigate around the system. There will always be a set of "buttons" at the bottom of the screen to help you, although not all of the buttons are illuminated all of the time. The fastest method of going directly to a section of Prodigy is with the use of "JUMP words." Simply click on the JUMP icon or press Control-J and then type in the name of the service you wish to go to. For instance, JUMP GENEALOGY will quickly take you to the Genealogy Bulletin Board on Prodigy. However, anyone using Prodigy at 2,400 baud will find it to be rather slow. The graphics screens can take quite some time to transmit at 2,400 baud. 9,600 baud is strongly recommended, and 14,400 baud is now available in some areas. Almost all of Prodigy's members are in North America.

Anyone experienced in other online systems who is a new member of Prodigy quickly notices two major differences:

➡ **Advertising** Prodigy derives a large part of its income from the sale of advertising. Ads appear on the bottom of many screens while online. However, the advertising does not appear when reading messages in the Bulletin Boards. At any time an advertisement is displayed you can click on the ad to obtain more information or to order the product. Prodigy is the only online service to include advertising in this manner, it is probably the best system for online shopping.

➔ **Files for Downloading**   There aren't any files in the various bulletin boards. Prodigy is the only online service with a genealogy section that offers absolutely no genealogy files for downloading. However, the Prodigy Internet gateway does allow for downloading files from online services other than Prodigy.

There is an excellent "offline message handler" available for Prodigy called the Bulletin Board Notes Manager for Windows, or BBNM for short. It can be directly downloaded from Prodigy for a one-time charge of $19.95; it will pay for itself many times over if you become a frequent visitor to Prodigy bulletin boards. The Bulletin Board Notes Manager allows you to log onto Prodigy and quickly capture all the messages in one or more bulletin boards. Once they are stored on your hard disk, it logs off and the online charges cease. You can then browse through the messages at your leisure without worrying about the amount of online charges being incurred. Likewise, composing replies and new messages can be done at your leisure; the program will send your new messages after you are finished.

One of the major advantages of the Bulletin Board Note Manager is that it circumvents all the on-screen advertisements. There are no ads displayed when using BBNM. However, there is no method of configuring BBNM to retrieve only message topics of interest—you must retrieve all messages on the Bulletin Board in order to read any of them. If you visit once a week or so, this will take about an hour at 9,600 baud for the Genealogy Bulletin Board alone.

A competitive "offline message handler" is available for both Windows and for MS-DOS computers although it is not produced by Prodigy. You can use JUMP ROYSTON for information about it.

Online Chats are popular on Prodigy and there is one chat room designated for use by genealogists. "Handles" or so-called screen names seem to be popular on Prodigy, you rarely know the name of the person you are chatting with. Some of the chat rooms are for "adults only" and the conversations there can indeed be for mature audiences only. Prodigy has an excellent system for parental control of access to those rooms.

If you need assistance with the use of Prodigy, you can call their Customer Service department at 1-800-PRODIGY. If you are online, you can obtain Customer Service assistance by clicking on Member Help Center on the first screen you see after logging on. That takes you to an area of Prodigy that is free of on-line charges.

Like all the other Bulletin Boards on Prodigy, the Genealogy BB is easy to use. Upon entering, you first see a welcoming screen written by Myra Vanderpool Gormley, Prodigy's resident "genealogy expert." Myra is a professional genealogist and noted syndicated columnist who writes "Shaking Your Family Tree." Myra is on the bulletin board frequently and often answers questions posed by members. Archives of past columns are available online and they may be printed directly or written to your local disk drive. John Seeley is listed as the "Genealogy Bulletin Board Leader" and he also often answers members' questions.

Prodigy's Genealogy Bulletin Board

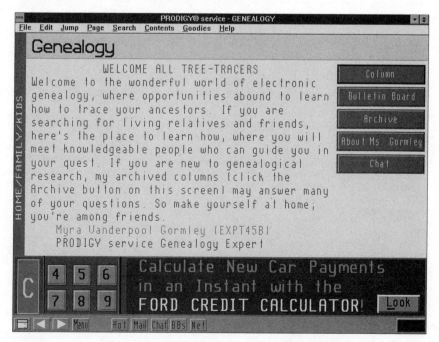

The Genealogy Bulletin Board consists of three main areas: Myra Vanderpool Gormley's columns, the message board, and an online chat area. There are no files available for downloading to your computer.

The Message Board   Prodigy's Genealogy Bulletin Board is divided into the following sections:

Adoption Research

African-American

Ancestor Archives

British Isles

Canada

Events & Freebies

Family Clubs/Newsletters

France

Germany

Hereditary Societies

Hispanic

Ireland

Italy & Sicily

Jewish

Military Sources

Missing—Alive

Native American

New Board Members

Other Countries

Poland

Reference

Royal/Noble/Heraldry

Scandinavia

Software & CDs

Surnames A-H

Surnames I-Z

U.S. Nat'l Resources

U.S. State Resources

Unclassified

The figure on the next page shows a sampling of Prodigy topics of interest. Each of these sections seems to have a lot of messages, in a recent week 4,142 new messages were posted to the Genealogy Bulletin Board according to the Bulletin Board Notes Manager. Messages may be addressed to a specific person or they may be broadcast "To: ALL." If you are involved in exchanging messages on the Genealogy Bulletin Board, you can enter select "See Notes only to Member ID" and then fill in your own Member ID in the box. That will allow you to quickly see any replies to your previously posted messages, which will be much faster and easier than manually searching through all the topics.

The messages on Prodigy's Genealogy Bulletin Board seem to cover a wide variety of genealogy-related topics. Message titles are automatically listed in alphabetical order, allowing quick and easy access to topics of interest. Messages from representatives of several genealogy-related companies are frequently found there.

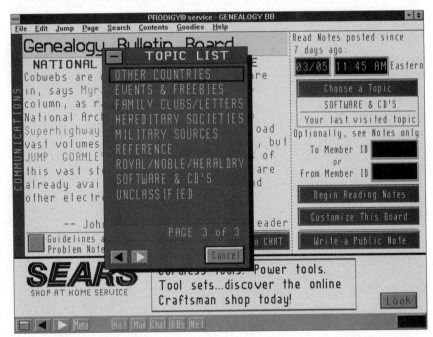

Sampling of Prodigy topics of interest

Files Despite the use of the phrase "bulletin board," Prodigy's bulletin boards lack the file transfer capabilities that other bulletin boards have. There are no genealogy-related files available for downloading other than Myra Gormley's weekly newsletters.

Chat Room There is one Chat Room associated with the Genealogy Bulletin Board and it can often be an interesting place to join other genealogists in live conversations. It is open 24 hours a day.

A typical message as seen while in interactive mode on Prodigy

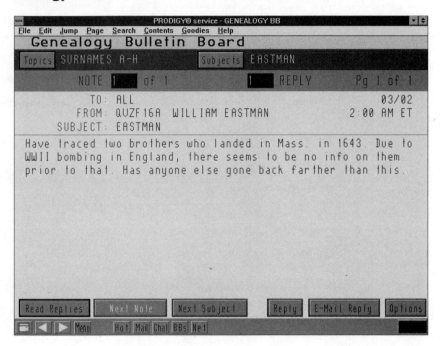

Prodigy's Internet Services All Prodigy members have access to genealogy information on the Internet services, including the World Wide Web, ftp, and Usenet Newsgroups. Prodigy does not provide Telnet capability yet, however. The information available through Prodigy's Internet gateways will be similar to that available through other Internet connections.

America Online

The newest commercial online service is America Online. This service first appeared a few years ago and has grown rapidly since. While it doesn't have as

The same message as seen in the Bulletin Board Notes Manager while offline

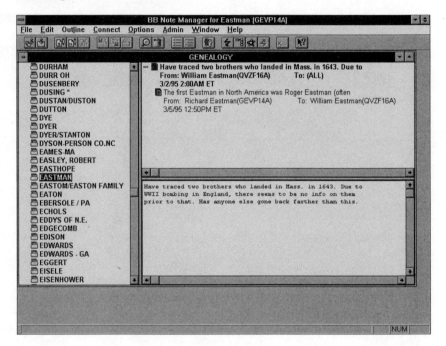

many different services available as its larger competitor, America Online has focused on offering home and hobbyist services. Their Genealogy Club is one of the more active sections available.

America Online's slick graphical interface is its strongest feature. Navigating around this online service is easy to do with their MS-DOS, Windows, or Macintosh software. America Online appears to be the easiest of all the online services to use because of the simplicity of their navigation software.

However, you must use America Online's software, there is no third-party software available. Owners of Amiga, UNIX, and older computer systems will not be able to access this online service. Automated communications programs are not generally available for America Online, you are normally restricted to typing live on the keyboard while online.

America Online's opening screen

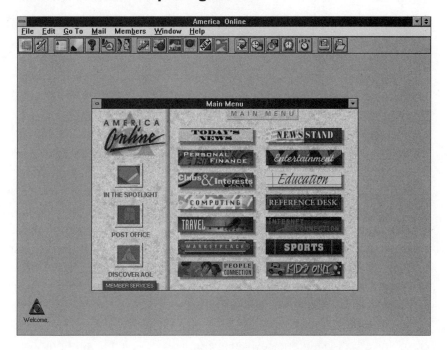

There are two exceptions to the requirement to type live on the keyboard:

E-mail can be quickly sent, received, and processed offline through the use of "FlashScripts." It is possible to log on, quickly grab all mail and then log off. You can read the mail and compose new messages while offline. The new messages can then be sent in a later online session. If you use e-mail a lot this feature can save a lot of online charges as you are not reading and composing messages while online with the meter running.

A shareware program called WHALE does add some scripting capability to AOL's regular software. This is a big help in reducing online time and charges although it is not as powerful as the free-standing automated communications programs available for some of the other online services.

America Online's e-mail service is similar to that of Prodigy's: You can send mail to other America Online members as well as to anyone with an Internet address. You can also send a fax to any fax machine.

America Online's pricing is very competitive. The base rate is $9.95 per month and that includes up to 5 hours of online time each month. Additional time is charged at $2.95 per hour. There are no services with unlimited free time available other than a few items related to America Online services, such as the ability to review one's charges.

Most members connect to America Online by dialing a Tymnet number or a SprintNet number. 9,600 baud access is commonly available in most cities, while rural areas are generally restricted to 2,400 baud. 14,400 baud can be used in most of the larger cities. America Online has purchased a network company and they are now starting to build their own communications network under the name AOLnet. Once completed, this network will allow 28,800 baud access. Most AOL members are in the United States and Canada. There are very few overseas members.

Anyone who uses AOL at 14,400 baud will find the interactive menus a pleasure to use with only frequent short delays while graphics screens get transferred to the local Macintosh or PC. However, anyone using 2,400 baud will spend a lot of time staring at the words "Please wait while we add new art to America Online" while navigating around the system.

America Online uses "screen names" that are reminiscent of the old CB Radio craze. Instead of using one's own name or a series of letters and numbers as a User ID, America Online members pick a "handle" of their own choice. If not already in use by another member, this "screen name" becomes the name by which the person is known online.

One significant difference in America Online's "culture" is the popularity of its chat areas. There are hundreds of online conference rooms. Some of the more popular chat rooms include Best Lil ChatHouse, Game Parlor, Gay and Lesbian, Thirtysomething, Over Forty, Romance Connection, The Flirts Nook, The Meeting Place, and Trivia. The conversations that take place in these more popular chat rooms usually reflect the room names.

While many of these chat rooms may resemble a singles bar, parental control is available for those people who allow their children to use their America Online accounts. On a typical evening each and every one of these chat rooms will be full of people engaged in live conversations. There are many other chat rooms

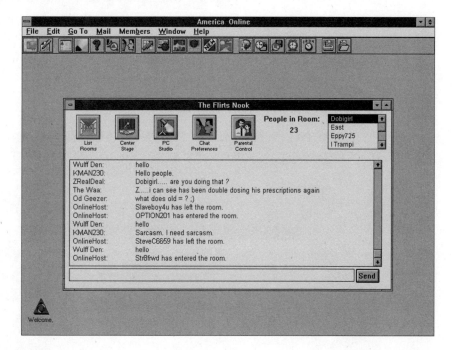

America Online chat session

devoted to specialized topics, including two chat rooms on the Genealogy Club that will be described later.

If you need assistance with the use of America Online, you can call their Customer Service department at 1-800-827-6364. If you are online, you can obtain Customer Service assistance by clicking on Customer Services on the first screen you see after logging on. That takes you to an area of America Online that is free of online charges.

The **Genealogy Club** is one of the more active sections on America Online. It is managed by George Ferguson, who uses a screen name of "GFL George." George is a professional genealogist who has worked with computers for over 20 years. He was one of the original founders of the Genealogy Club. The information bulletins also list a number of other assistants: GFA Terry is a Librarian in a Family History Library, GFA Drew is a professor with expertise in the Internet side of Genealogy, and GFA Beth handles the more than 3,500 files in the Genealogy File library with help from GFA Robin and GFS Jeff. The Club's information bulletins also list "Assistant-Hosts" GFA Rebel and GFA Maureen.

➡ *Genealogy Club help screen*

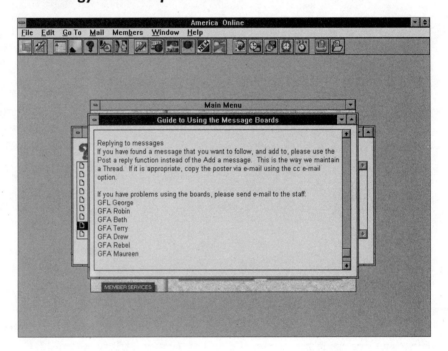

Message Board   The most active section of the Genealogy Club is its message board. The message board is divided into five categories. Each category has up to 50 topics, called "folders." Each topic has up to 500 messages, each message can have as many as 500 replies or responses.

On the Genealogy Club messages are not allowed to be posted to specific individuals. In effect, all messages are simply broadcast to everyone. The downside of this is that if someone replies to your message the only way to find that reply is to go back through all the sections and to look for it. There is no automatic notification of waiting new messages intended for you when you enter the Genealogy Club. Most experienced members write down the titles and sections of the message they post so that they will know where to look for replies on subsequent visits. The message board information advises that "If your response will be of interest only to one person, then please send e-mail instead of posting a reply."

The Message Area is divided into the following sections:

- **States**   New area to put genealogical information and queries about your ancestors that came from specific states.

- **General Genealogy**   An area to exchange helpful hints with one another. In the noncomputer areas of Genealogy, this is also a place to look for what's happening in the club and around the country.

- **Computer Tools & Techniques**   An area to discuss the computerized topics in Genealogy.

- **Surnames**   This is a place to post your queries about the people you are researching. The folders are in alphabetical order and within each folder are surnames others are researching.

- **People, Places, and Times**   This is a place to exchange information about people that came from similar places and/or times.

Navigating through the message board is easy. The "Find New" command is the best method of finding all the new messages posted since your last visit. "List All" will show all messages on the message board, regardless of dates. It is easy to create a new topic as well.

One of the more useful areas of the Message Board is the Surname Message Area. This area is set up with a folder for each letter of the alphabet. Within each folder you will find a listing of surnames that start with that letter. The result is that you can communicate with others researching the same surnames by adding to the message thread for that name.

A sample message board

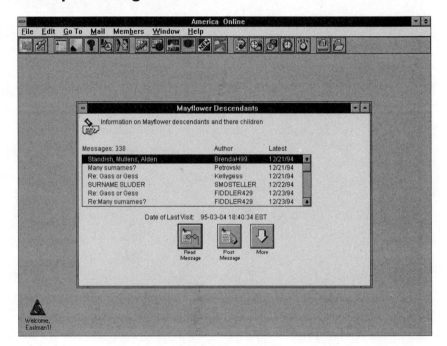

Chat Rooms   There are two **chat rooms** on the Genealogy Club: the Ancestral Digs and Golden Gates conference halls. Like the other chat rooms on AOL, these are very popular and online conferences happen there on most evenings. These two rooms seem to have more "serious" conversations than the socially oriented rooms mentioned earlier. General meetings are held twice a week in the Genealogy chart rooms on Sunday and Thursday nights. They also hold meetings of Special Interest groups throughout the week for those doing research in specific areas and ethnic groups. A full listing of scheduled chats is easily found online.

Files Available   The Genealogy Club has more than 3,500 files available that may be transferred across the telephone lines at once and stored on a local hard drive. The file section is divided into 15 areas:

1. Macintosh files

2. MSDOS files

3. Research Tips

4. Genealogical Records

5. Surname Archives

6. Ethnic and Regional Archives

7. GEDCOM 1

8. GEDCOM 2

9. Tiny Tafels

10. Ahnentafels

11. Lineage 1

12. Lineage 2

13. Logs of past meetings

14. Lectures—Copies of the lectures given in the SIGs

15. Graphics

Finding files on AOL is easy with their menu systems. Also, files are fully described before downloading. In the figure, the file FT4WIN.ZIP is described as "Family Tree for Windows." This file will require about 19 minutes to download at 9,600 baud, and it has been downloaded 635 times previously.

Family Tree for Windows

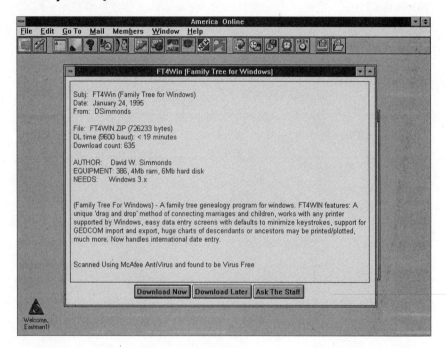

Clicking on the "Download Now" button initiates the file transfer. All binary files on America Online's Genealogy Club have been checked for viruses before being made available to everyone.

Internet   All America Online members have some access to genealogy information on the Internet services, primarily through Usenet Newsgroups and ftp. AOL doesn't provide either World Wide Web or ftp capabilities yet, however. The UseNet and ftp information available through AOL's Internet gateways will be similar to that available through other Internet connections.

The Internet

Describing the Internet can sometimes be an exercise in frustration. There is no clear definition of just what the Internet is and isn't. The easiest method of describing it is to say that the Internet is the largest computer network in the world. But even that definition is technically incorrect; it is not so much a single network as it is a network of networks. That is, it is multiple computer networks hooked together through gateways. The exact number of computers accessible through the Internet is unknown but the number is apparently in the hundreds of thousands. The amount of information that travels along this so-called "information superhighway" is too large to ever be measured.

Major newspapers and popular magazines are full of articles about the Internet and the supposed riches that are there. Most of these articles are factual, but many are written in such glowing terms that they insinuate that any piece of information you could ever want can be obtained on the Internet. While this simplistic view may become a reality in the twenty-first century, it will not happen before then.

For the genealogist who imagines huge databases of vital records, military pension records, ships' passenger lists and other records vital to genealogy research, disappointment arrives early. Most such records have never been computerized. Still, there is a great deal of information and assistance of value to the genealogist on the Internet. This section will identify the more valuable ones.

The Internet is the most open computer network in the world; anyone can obtain access to it. Many people can obtain access at their place of work or at the college they attend as the fees are paid by the employer or are bundled into tuition and student fees. Anyone without such access can still easily gain Internet access from any of the major online services, such as CompuServe, Prodigy, or America Online. Also, many smaller and often local "Internet providers" offer access to anyone for a sign-up fee and a monthly rate or an hourly rate. All it takes is a modem and a bit of software.

The Internet provides e-mail, information retrieval, the ability to operate remote databases, and a kind of bulletin board system called Usenet News Groups. Almost anyone who has an e-mail system on a computer can send and receive nternet mail, access to the other services (Telnet, ftp, and World Wide Web) varies widely.

~💻~

The "roots" of Internet started in ARPANET, a project started by the Department of Defense in 1969 to link researchers together in an electronic mail system for those doing government-funded military research. The original ARPANET connected four computers together and others were quickly added. Some years later the project was taken over by the National Science Foundation for access to their proposed supercomputer projects. Again, the purpose of the network was for government-funded research. As the network became larger and more flexible, other purposes "slipped in" until it no longer was a research-only network. Then more and more "commercialization" of the Internet appeared and government funding was slowly reduced every year as commercial companies took over more of the funding. The funding by the government, particularly that of the National Science Foundation, is now a tiny fraction of what it once was. Most of the network itself is provided by large corporations such as Sprint and IBM, as well as some specialized companies whose sole purpose is to provide Internet access.

~💻~

If your employer or school can provide Internet access at little or no cost to you, that will be the preferred method. While nothing on the Internet is really free, having one's employer pay the cost of computers, software, high-speed lines, and so on can make it appear to be free to the individual. You might want to enlist the assistance of a knowledgeable coworker, as plunging into Internet access software can be a daunting task for the unprepared.

Many small companies have appeared in the last few years that provide Internet access for a fee. These are usually local companies although there are a few larger ones. Probably the most convenient of the Internet providers is Sprint with their SprintLink service. This service is available anywhere in the U.S. for $8.95 per month plus $8.95 per hour. This is one of the higher-priced Internet providers, but it is available in rural areas that may not have any other Internet access. It can also be useful to the person who travels a lot as you can access SprintLink from any location.

Most local Internet providers will charge between $10 to $30 per month for normal dial-up access and will bundle in some number of hours as well with additional hours billed accordingly. A local company that I have used charges $29 per month and includes 40 hours of online time bundled in. This includes full SLIP and PPP access (more about those acronyms later). They also have a customer support department that answers phone calls 7 days a week. There are other local companies that will provide limited Internet access or a smaller number of bundled hours for prices as low as $10 per month. The amount and quality of customer support available from these companies varies widely.

Finally, anyone with access to the major commercial online systems such as CompuServe, Prodigy, or America Online also has access to the Internet. CompuServe provides full PPP, ftp, Telnet, and World Wide Web access with prices as low as 75 cents per hour. The other services have most of the same Internet services and have announced plans to add the remainder. The major commercial online systems provide several advantages, such as much more user-friendly software that is easy to install and use, a customer support department available both online and by voice at an 800 number, and the ability to be used via local access numbers while traveling. They typically are a bit more expensive than the smaller Internet access providers, however.

This section could fill an entire book by itself. Indeed, there are over 100 books available today at most large book stores that are devoted to the Internet. For technical details, you should refer to those.

The Internet runs mostly on Unix systems along with a mixture of DEC VAXes, IBM mainframes, OS/2 microcomputers, and probably many other operating systems as well. Early PC and Macintosh software designed to work with the Internet forced the user to learn syntax not normally found in personal systems. However, the new generation of Internet software available now for Microsoft Windows, OS/2, and for the Macintosh has greatly improved useability. It is now possible to navigate through much of the Internet by simply clicking a mouse at the appropriate times; it is no longer necessary to memorize strange syntax for Unix commands and funny TCP/IP addresses, or to worry about uppercase and lowercase naming conventions.

The software required on your PC or Macintosh depends upon the type of connection you have to the Internet. In some cases all you need is simple terminal emulation software as you dial into a host machine elsewhere and the host provides the Internet access. More sophisticated software, such as Mosaic, allows your computer to become a part of the network itself. To accomplish this you need to become familiar with terminology like packet drivers, TCP/IP addresses, SLIP (Serial Line Internet Protocol) and PPP (Point to Point Protocol). A technical discussion of all this is outside the scope of this genealogy book but you can obtain detailed information on all of this online or at any bookstore.

In all cases you will have to connect to a "service provider" who then provides you with access to the Internet. All software required for your Macintosh or PC can be obtained directly from those companies and is quickly and easily installed. The examples in this book will show Internet access as seen through Mosaic software on CompuServe's Internet gateways, but access through other Internet providers will generally look quite similar.

One subject that cannot be totally ignored is that of addresses. Just as every person and company has a postal address to which you can send letters and packages, every computer (or "node") on the Internet has an address. While these are based on a series of numbers called TCP/IP addresses, most of them are also translated into somewhat more friendly looking strings of letters and numbers. There is no master directory of all the Internet addresses; you normally have to ask someone for their address first before you can send e-mail to them. In the case of the larger online databases and other services, the addresses are published in many places in print and online.

An Internet e-mail address usually starts with the person's logon ID on his or her local system followed by an @ sign (meaning "at") and then the electronic address for that local computer system. For instance, these are typical e-mail addresses:

john.smith@bigcorp.com

jsmith@dept.bigcorp.com

76701.263@compuserve.com

GEVP14A@prodigy.com

mlwalker@lynx.neu.edu

eastman@tiac.net

president@whitehouse.gov

sjohnson@dis.mil

Notice the last three letters. Each is a designator for the type of organization: com stands for commercial companies, edu stands for an educational institution, net is for someone who is a part of the network, gov indicates a government computer, and mil is for a military address. Those conventions are common throughout the United States although there may be variations elsewhere. In addition, there are optional suffixes to indicate county. An address ending in ".fr" would be in France, ".uk" would be in the United Kingdom and ".jp" would be in Japan.

When accessing other computers directly that are on the same system that you are, no user ID or @ is required.

The decentralization and diversity of the Internet provides many unique problems that do not exist on the mainframe-based online systems. There is no directory of electronic addresses. Also there is no master list of what information is available. All information is dispersed throughout the world and changes frequently. Just attempting to find some piece of information that you want can be a frustrating experience. Every company that owns a computer service available via the Internet is free to do whatever they believe is best. There is little standardization and no central repository of assistance. There is no Customer Support department available with an 800 telephone number. The Internet user is expected to do his or her own technical support.

"Network loading" can also be a frequent problem. When many people are trying to access one point on the network bottlenecks can and frequently do occur. Even though you are using a 28,800 baud modem it is not uncommon to sit and stare at a screen that shows little activity because of some peak useage out in the network. The more popular the source you are trying to reach, the more likely you will find delays. Attempting to connect to any of the bigger ftp sites on a weekday evening will often generate a message about "maximum number of users already signed on, try again later."

Even with these minor drawbacks, navigating through the Internet can be a rewarding experience. Even experienced "net surfers" find new information every day on the Internet.

The commands used to send and receive electronic mail (e-mail) vary widely. In most cases, the local mail system already installed on the host computer can send and receive Internet mail simply by specifying a proper address. For instance, in CompuServe Mail you specify an address of ">INTERNET:" followed by the regular Internet address and the regular mail system takes care of the routing. You can receive Internet mail in exactly the same manner as any other mail. The same is true on most mainframe and minicomputer e-mail systems.

Delivery of e-mail throughout the Internet normally occurs within a few minutes although a few smaller systems may not be directly connected to the Internet. These systems typically will dial into the network periodically to send and receive stored mail.

Privacy of e-mail on the Internet is not guaranteed. Due to the huge volume of mail that passes through the network every day, the odds of someone looking at your message are small but there still remains some risk. "Network sniffers" are sophisticated tools that exist in almost all major switching points along the network, most of these can be programmed to search for credit card numbers or logon IDs and passwords. Network "hackers" have used these tools to obtain confidential information. Never send a credit card number through the Internet, and change your passwords often.

Some of the earliest Internet "bulletin boards" first existed as mailing lists. In this case, an e-mail message was sent to an electronic address, software at the receiving end would then forward copies of that e-mail message to the mailboxes of everyone on the "subscription list." Many thousands of these mailing lists exist today, they are simple to set up and administer and usually do not require a lot of permissions on the host system. The disadvantage of mailing lists is that the more popular ones can flood your electronic mailbox with hundreds of messages every day.

There are many mailing lists devoted to genealogy topics. A few families even have their own mailing lists as a method of having "family newsletters" of who is doing what. The most popular genealogy mailing list is called ROOTS-L. To subscribe to it, send an e-mail message to: **listserv@vm1.nodak.edu** and the entire text of the message should be: **SUBSCRIBE ROOTS-L firstname lastname** where you substitute your own first and last names.

Some of the other genealogy-related mailing lists include the following:

AAGENE-L—Discussions of African American genealogy. To subscribe, send e-mail to aagene-l@upeople.com with SUBSCRIBE as the subject.

CLACAMPB@FREENET.FSU.EDU—A mailing list for Campbell descendants to discuss their possible kinship and for Clan Campbell to try to get members. To become a part of this group, send e-mail to clacampb@freenet.fsu.edu.

COOLEY-L—Researchers of the surname COOLEY. To subscribe, send a request to be added to the list to cooley-l-request@genealogy.emcee.com.

GEN-DE-L—newsgroup for the discussion of German genealogy. To subscribe, send the following to listserv@nz11.rz.uni-karlsruhe.de: SUB GEN-DE-L firstname lastname

GEN-FF-L—newsgroup for the discussion of Francophone genealogy—the genealogy of French-speaking people (traffic probably mainly in French). To subscribe, send the following to listserv@gitvm1.gatech.edu: SUB GEN-FF-L firstname lastname

GEN-FR-L—group for the discussion of Francophone genealogy—the genealogy of French-speaking people (traffic probably mainly in English). To subscribe, send the following to listserv@gitvm1.gatech.edu: SUBSCRIBE GEN-FR-L firstname lastname

GENCMP-L—newsgroup for the discussion of genealogical computing and net resources. To subscribe, send the following to listserv@gitvm1.gatech.edu: SUBSCRIBE GENCMP-L firstname lastname

GENMSC-L—newsgroup for general genealogical discussions that don't fit within one of the other soc.genealogy.* newsgroups. To subscribe, send the following to listserv@gitvm1.gatech.edu: SUBSCRIBE GENMSC-L firstname lastname

GENMTD-L—newsgroup for the discussion of genealogy methods and resources. To subscribe, send the following to listserv@gitvm1.gatech.edu: SUBSCRIBE GENMTD-L firstname lastname

GENNAM-L—newsgroup for surname queries and tafels. To subscribe, send the following to listserv@gitvm1.gatech.edu: SUBSCRIBE GENNAM-L firstname lastname

GER-RUS—Germans from Russia. To subscribe, send the following to listserv@vm1.nodak.edu: SUBSCRIBE GER-RUS firstname lastname

JEWGEN—Discussions of Jewish genealogy. To subscribe, send the following to listserv@gitvm1.gatech.edu: SUBSCRIBE JEWGEN firstname lastname

KYROOTS—Discussions of Kentucky genealogical and historical research. To subscribe, send the following to listserv@ukcc.uky.edu: SUBSCRIBE KYROOTS firstname lastname

LYMAN-L—researchers of the surname LYMAN. To subscribe, send a request to be added to the list to request@genealogy.emcee.com.

There are many more such mailing lists and the complete listing changes constantly. An updated listing can be found on almost all the online services that allow for file transfers. Also, SRI maintains a "list of lists" that you can obtain via e-mail. Simply send an e-mail message to: mail-server@nisc.sri.com and use this line of text in the body of hte message: send netinfo/interest-groups.

Mailing lists came first but quickly became inefficient as a method of sending messages to thousands of people. If a mailing list goes to 5,000 people and has 200 messages per day, the amount of e-mail load can overtax many systems. Usenet News or NetNews solves that by creating news articles and then shipping copies of the articles to nearby computers. Each of these computers forwards copies to more computers and, within a very few hours, messages posted to the newsgroups are available worldwide. In operation these NewsGroups look quite similar to forums on the mainframe systems and also similar to bulletin board systems that run on PCs. However, Newsgroups do not provide the capability to download files.

All messages are posted to the group at large, it is not possible to post a message to one individual and ensure that he or she will be notified when entering the newsgroup. (Use e-mail for messages directed to one person.) Most large Unix systems, most local Internet providers, and all the major commercial online services now carry Usenet Newsgroups.

Navigating though these newsgroups can be a bit intimidating as there are so many topics available. Usenet has more than 8,000 newsgroups ranging from alt.genealogy to alt.binaries.pictures.erotica.bestiality. There are probably 100 or so newsgroups devoted to pornography and to sexual behavior "outside the socially acceptable norms of the majority of the population," so you might be cautious about giving your adolescent child unlimited access to newsgroups or other Internet services.

Newsgroups come in two different varieties: moderated and unmoderated. The moderated newsgroups have a person or a group of people who keep an eye on the messages there and generally control the newsgroup. Unmoderated newsgroups have no one in charge and the messages in those can vary widely. Anyone may post any message to unmoderated newsgroups.

Out of the 8,000+ Usenet Newsgroups available, the following are devoted to genealogy-related topics (and this list will probably expand):

alt.genealogy

alt.scottish.clans

fr.rec.genealogie (all messages are usually in French)

soc.genealogy.computing (genealogical computing methods)

soc.genealogy.french (larger group—messages in both French and English)

soc.genealogy.german (German genealogy— messages in both English and German)

soc.genealogy.methods (genealogy research methods)

soc.genealogy.misc (anyting that doesn't fit into the other soc.gene* groups)

soc.genealogy.jewish

soc.genealogy.surnames (surname queries, tiny tafels)

The most widely used interactive Internet services are the various types of Telnet remote logins. Telnet has been described as "The next best thing to being there." Telnet is the primary method of searching library card catalogs, it is also used on many large databases. In short, Telnet is a method of logging onto a remote computer and running programs just as if you were using a local terminal at the computer site itself. In order to run a program on a remote computer, you first open a Telnet session to that system and then log on with a User ID and password (often publicly available) and then run the program as you would if you were in the same building with the computer.

Telnet is one of the older services available on the Internet. The local screen and keyboard on your PC or Macintosh becomes a terminal connected to a computer hundreds or even thousands of miles away. It is easy to run Telnet sessions to run programs on computers in Sweden or Australia or almost anyplace else in the world. Almost all the smaller Internet provider companies allow Telnet access, as does CompuServe. However, Prodigy and America Online members cannot use Telnet yet.

Many computer systems allow "guest logins" by publishing User IDs and passwords. These User IDs normally have very limited power, usually only the capability to run a database search. Many of the library online card catalog systems don't even ask for a User ID. When a remote system does ask for a logon, the most common one is "*anonymous*" with a password equivalent to your e-mail address. This will connect you to thousands of computers around the world.

One interesting note is that it is possible to establish a Telnet session to CompuServe and access any of CompuServe's many services. A CompuServe User ID and password are still required, of course. This is a great benefit to anyone in rural areas or in other parts of the world where high-speed CompuServe access may not be available but Internet access is. The personnel at the U.S. base at the

South Pole regularly use Telnet to access CompuServe as there is no local CompuServe dialup number there!

Genealogists will quickly learn the power of searching online library card catalogs. Almost all of these require Telnet access. A few other items of interest to
genealogists are also available via Telnet. Among the computers of interest to genealogists that can be accessed by telent sessions are the following:

Library of Congress—locis.loc.gov, Access code: Telnet

British Columbia Archives and Records Services—freenet.victoria.bc.ca (login: guest)

California State Library, University of California—melvyl.ucop.edu

Canadian National Archives (Carleton College Freenet)—freenet.carleton.ca
(login: guest)

Chicano Research Collection (Hayden Library, Arizona State University,
Tempe, Arizona; secondary and primary source materials on Mexican Americans
and Chicanos) carl.lib.asu.edu (access library)—info.lib.asu.edu (access database
server)

Colorado Alliance of Research Libraries—pac.carl.org (type PAC)

GALIN Catalog (University of Georgia)—ibm.cc.uga.edu

Geographic Name Server (provides city, county, state/province, nation, telephone area code, elevation, feature, lat/long, 1980 population, remarks, time
zone, zip code)—martini.eecs.umich.edu 3000

KANSAS (Heritage will include family histories (pioneers...), Kansas Pioneers
Project, local histories (schools, towns...), Kansas One-Room School Houses
Project, Historical Directory of Kansas Towns, list of Kansas Genealogical and
Historical Societies), Kansas On-Line (The Information Server for Kansas History
and Life)—ukanaix.cc.ukans.edu (login: history)

Heritage (The Center for Kansas Genealogy and Family and Local History)—
ukanaix.cc.ukans.edu (login: heritage)

Library of Michigan—libofmich.lib.mi.us (login: answer)

Minnesota Libraries and Minnesota Historical Society—pals.msus.edu
(searching commands: menu)

Mirlyn Card Catalog (University of Michigan)—mirlyn.telnet.lib.umich.edu
(terminal only) mirlyn.lib.umich.edu (for tn3270 and tcp3270)

New York City Public Library (largest collections in Jewish and Genealogy Divisions)—nyplgate.nypl.org (login: nypl)

Vesterheim Museum Library for Norwegian-American History. Once connected, type "PAC" (without quotes) and choose terminal type. Then go to Other Libraries (4), Western US Libraries (43), Luther College Network (132),Vesterheim Museum Library—pac.carl.org

VLIN (Virginia Library Information Network?)—hp3000.vsla.edu (login: hello gopher,ref.clas52)

This list is updated constantly, the latest versions can be found on almost all the online systems that support file transfers.

 ### An example of a library card catalog search

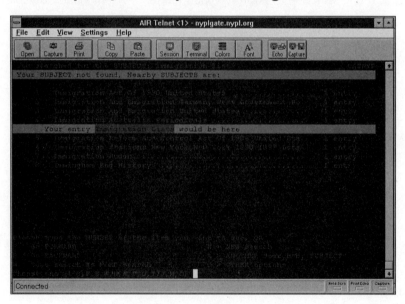

~🖳~

Ftp is another one of the earlier services available on the Internet. It simply is a method of copying files from one computer to another. Typically this means copying a file from a remote system to your PC or Macintosh, although it is equally easy to transfer files in the opposite direction. Originally ftp required the use of Unix-style commands. Changing subdirectories required forward slashes instead of backslashes and the command to list the files stored there was *ls* instead of the DIR command that MS-DOS users were accustomed to. Of course, all this was even more confusing to Macintosh users.

Today's software has taken the mystique out of all this. However, you still need to be aware that file names on remote systems are normally case sensitive. MYFILE.TXT, myfile.txt, Myfile.txt, Myfile.TXT and MyFiLe.TxT are all different files! Also, many files have longer names than are allowed in MS-DOS and they may have more than one period in the file name. Myfile.txt.Z is a legal file name on most remote systems. The ftp software that you use in your PC or Macintosh will translate these names into something compatible with your system.

There are many archives of files available throughout the Internet. The bigger systems may have hundreds of users on at one time and therefore can be overloaded. Smaller systems may have sections devoted to the interests that you have, such as genealogy, and not have as much of a load. These file archives are created from many sources and managed in many different ways. Some of the better-managed systems have system mangers who work hard at keeping the latest revisions of all software on file and ensuring that each file is checked for viruses before becoming available to everyone. Other sites may not be as well managed, viruses may exist at some sites. Always be cautious about using any file that you obtain via ftp on the Internet.

Another issue is legality: Just because a file is available someplace does not mean that it is legal for you to obtain it and use it. The U.S. court systems are just beginning to learn about computer case law so it is difficult to make blanket statements about what is legal and what is not. However, copies of commercial software programs do exist on the Internet without permission of the producers, text files that are clearly labeled as copyrighted works also circulate. If you should obtain such materials, you might think twice before passing them on to others. The majority of system administrators are very conscientious about this and want to be notified of any questionable files on their systems. You can normally send an e-mail message to: postmaster@<site-name> to notify them.

Again, you can log onto systems that allow anonymous logins. The most common method is to use a User ID of *"anonymous"* and a password consisting of your e-mail address. The following systems allow anonymous logins and have files of interest to genealogists:

ftp.cac.psu.edu—Many subdirectories including Personal Ancestral File, GEDCOM, genealogy programs and utilitiess, ROOTS-L archives, and others

vm1.nodak.edu—ROOTS-L files

oak.oakland.edu—various genealogy software

ftp.netcom.com—look in directory: pub/GS/GSDS for the Genealogy Software Distribution System

ftp.xmission.com—look in directory: pub/users/jayhall for Windows genealogy programs; an index of British, German, and Loyalist officers in the American Revolution; Everton's catalog, catalog for Automated Archives, and so on

coombs.anu.edu.au (in Australia)—look in directory: coombspapers/otherarchives/uk-nra-archives for: Research guides from the UK National Register of Archives. Includes files dealing with genealogy, colonial history, family history, and so on—all of which have extensive source bibliographies, hints on conducting genealogy research, and useful addresses

solb1.essex.ac.uk (in England)—look in directory: pub/genealogy for files from the 2 percent sample of the 1851 UK Census

gateway.census.gov—Many subdirectories for various subjects including genealogy. Contains 80 register page images (TIFF files) from the 1900 and 1910 censuses of Greenville and Greenwood Counties, South Carolina, found in pub/genealogy/images

ftp.loc.gov—U.S. Library of Congress

genealogy.emcee.com—Many subdirectories including vendors/nqf (issues of The National Queries Forum), vendors/sq (surname index for Southern Queries Magazine, file sq.zip), groups (list of genealogical societies, file groups.txt.zip), surnames (information on COOLEY, PETTIT and ASHENHURST), software. Also includes 1% sampling of the 1880 Federal census.

rtfm.mit.edu—U.S. Civil War reading list

nmdpow9.er.usgs.gov—Text file of 154,000 U.S. populated-place names from USGS Geographic Names Information System

ftp.mindspring.com—Information on Global Heritage Center, a commercial enterprise with genealogy CD-ROMs

The one Internet "service" that has the most appeal is the World Wide Web (WWW), a rather new piece of software that allows hypertext links connecting information on multiple computers. The Web is really more *hypermedia* than it is hypertext, as graphics and sound clips can be embedded within text documents.

In short, you may browse through a *Web page* on one computer and see a reference to George Washington. The words "George Washington" may be highlighted in a different color; clicking on those words will then display detailed information on George. That information may actually be stored on the same computer or on another computer in a different part of the world. The "linking" of this information is almost transparent to the user.

Since any World Wide Web page can link to any other World Wide Web page in the universe, you will find hundreds of pages that are lists or indexes of where to find information. As you read the list, you can move the mouse and click on anything listed and you are then connected to the Web page listed even if it is located on a different host.

World Wide Web addresses may look unusual even to the experienced Internet user. All addresses start with the letters *http* (meaning HyperText Transfer Protocol) or *gopher* (stands for "*go for*" that uses lists found on other servers) followed by a colon, two slashes and then the address of the computer. The following list shows a few of the available World Wide Web pages of interest to genealogists:

Association for Gravestone Studies: http://www.history.rochester.edu/ags/ags.html

Canadian National Archives, Carleton College Freenet: http://www.ncf.carleton.ca/

CompuSerrve: http://compuserve.com/index.html (enter "genealogy" when asked for a topic)

Dallas Virtual Jewish Community Center Genealogy Home Page: http://129.119.19.103/dvjcc/dvjcc.genealogy.html

Everton Publishers: http://www.xmission.com/~jayhall/

Genealogy Online: http://genealogy.emcee.com

GenTech (Genealogy Technology): http://www.gentech.org/~steele

GenWeb (Genealogy on WWW): http://irpsbbs.ucsd.edu/gene/gene-demo.html

Georgia Genealogical Information: http://www.mindspring.com/~bevr/bevr.html

German Nobility Index: http://faui80.informatik.uni-erlangen.de/html/ww-person.html

Germany/Russia, Odessa, a German-Russian Genealogy library: http://pixel.cs.vt.edu/library/odessa.html

Index to Genealogical WWW Pages: http://www.tic.com/gen.html

Ireland, North of Ireland Family History Society: http://www.os.qub.ac.uk/nifhs

Kentucky Vital Statistics (1911-1989): http://www.uky.edu

Library catalogs from around the U.S.: http://www.cc.ukans.edu/hytelnet_html/US000.html

Library of Congress: http://lcweb.loc.gov/homepage/lchp.html (WWW server)

Maps Can Help You Trace Your Family Tree: http://info.er.usgs.gov/fact-sheets/genealogy/index.html

Minnesota State University Minnesota Historical Society: http://garnet.msen.com:70/Oh/vendor/maven/mn/mn.html#lib

New Brunswick Genealogical Information: http://www.unb.ca/genealogy/nb-gen.html

Oregon State Archives: http://159.121.28.251

Prodigy: http://antares.prodigy.com/welcome.html

Silicon Valley PAF Users Group Home Page: http://www.rahul.net:80/svpafug/

U.S. Bureau of the Census Home Page: http://www.census.gov

U.S. National Archives and Records Administration: http://www.nara.gov

US Geographic Name Server: http://caesar.cs.uiowa.edu/cgi-bin/geographic-name-server

WWW Genealogy Demo Page: http://ftp.cac.psu.edu/~saw/genealogy.html

Many of the above World Wide Web pages will point to other pages on other systems. In addition, larger and frequently updated lists of genealogy-related Web pages can be obtained from practically all of the online genealogy services that support file transfers.

The one thing that you will notice about WWW is that it is really slow. The transfer of graphics files and sound clips requires passing thousands of bytes of information. Most Web browsers allow you to turn off the display of graphics; this increases performance although the resulting screens are not as attractive. Use of a 28,800 baud connection will still result in frequent delays of 30 to 60 seconds while receiving new pages. When the network is heavily loaded you may encounter even longer delays. Some companies are experimenting with sending full-motion video but that normally requires even higher speeds to be practical.

Bulletin Board Systems

Bulletin Board Systems are almost the exact opposite of the commercial online systems in many ways. Most bulletin board systems, or BBSs, are privately owned by one individual and are run as a hobby. These systems typically have one or two telephone lines connected and therefore can accommodate only one or two users at one time. There are exceptions, however. Some bulletin board systems may have in excess of 100 telephone lines connected and may run on a network of interconnected PCs. These are normally commercially owned and operated on a fee basis. Probably less than 1% of all BBSs are this large, however.

BBSs may be free of charge to users, with the owner paying for all the hardware and telephone fees. However, the more serious BBSs will often charge a fee for usage in order to help the owner defray the expenses. It is not unusual for both free and fee-based systems to carry the same or similar information, so shopping around to see what is available in your area is advised. You will probably encounter busy signals often when dialing free BBSs, however.

The "seriousness" of BBSs varies widely. The ones that will be discussed here are generally used by genealogists who are adults and are serious about using online systems. However, not all BBSs are managed in that manner. Many are owned and operated by adolescents and the message boards there will reflect the tastes of a different crowd. You may want to try a number of BBSs in your area in order to find the one that is right for you.

The popularity of BBSs has somewhat diminished since the explosive growth of the varied Internet services. Internet and BBSs are quite similar in operation and are often competing for the same audience. Internet typically offers a large network instantly accessible, a more immediate response, and a larger audience. However, the simplicity of setting up a BBS in one's home is still very attractive to many computer hobbyists, and BBSs will probably be around for many years yet.

BBSs originally served only those individuals who dialed directly to them, normally serving members within local calling range. However, a system of *echoes* has been established where one BBS will collect the messages posted to it and forward those to other BBSs. It will also collect messages from those other systems. Within a few days the messages that you enter on your local BBS may appear on other BBSs around the world. Anyone who replies to your message will similarly have their message appear on your local BBS within a few more days. These echoes are grouped by topics of interest, several genealogy echoes are available on BBSs around the world.

Unlike the centrally managed and controlled commercial online systems, BBSs operate in a distributed fashion. Control over message content is provided by the BBS owners (called "sysops") if they care to do so. Some sysops take a very active role in the management of their messages, while others do not. Many owners of the smaller BBSs carry only a few echoes reflecting the interests of the owner. Larger BBSs may have hundreds or even thousands of such echoes with the owner being simply unable to monitor what happens in each and every one.

The same will be true for customer support: that will depend upon the interest and the time available for the BBS owner to help his or her users.

Most BBSs will have files available for downloading. Again, based upon the owner's interests and time available, these may be large repositories of genealogy files or then again the local BBS may have no genealogy files available at all. Unlike the commercial online systems, virus infections are a major problem on BBSs. You should never download a file from a hobbyist's BBS and use it without doing an extensive virus check on it first.

Many BBSs automatically make all new files visible to everyone without any manual checks being made by the sysop. Some BBSs will automatically run a virus "scanner" on newly uploaded files that will trap most of the more common viruses, but these systems can easily be fooled by the more sophisticated viruses that appear today.

Some multiline BBSs may have the capability for one person to chat live on-line with another person, but this is limited only to those dialing to the same BBS. There is no method of having live chats with others around the world in the manner that is commonly done on the larger commercial online systems.

Most BBSs may be accessed by almost any regular communications program. The BBS software in use on different systems varies widely, each will have its own "look and feel." Automated "offline readers" are common also as most BBSs either limit the access of each user to certain number of minutes per day or else charge a fee for online time. Use of an "offline reader" allows for more information to be transferred in a shorter period of time.

Automated communications programs operate under the philosophy that a computer can always enter commands faster and more efficiently than a human being. Almost all of these automated programs operate in such a manner that a human never touches the keyboard while the computer is communicating with the BBS. The BBS normally bundles many messages together and then does a file transfer of them to the remote computer which stores the information on the local disk drive and then logs off. All the messages may then be read at your leisure.

Most of these automated communications programs also include mini word processors that you use for composing new messages. Again, you compose all messages offline at your leisure, you may stop and look up information as you wish. You may compose any number of messages offline.

Once all offline operations are completed, the remote computer dials back to the BBS and sends all the new information at maximum modem speed and then disconnects. Total online time may only be a minute or two. These BBS offline readers operate in a similar manner to the programs available for CompuServe and Prodigy although they will be different programs.

BBS "echoes" are easy to start. Therefore you can find quite a few available on various systems. The more popular ones are on the "Fidonet echoes" although a few exist elsewhere as well. The largest one runs under the guidance of the National Genealogical Society and is informally known as "the NGS echo." You do not need to be a member of NGS to participate, however.

Finding a bulletin board near you that carries the genealogy echoes may require some investigation on your part. One method is to use your computer and modem to dial long distance to the National Genealogical Society's BBS in Virginia. Once connected and registered, you can download a list of several hundred BBSs in the U.S. and many others around the world. You will probably find one in either your immediate dialing area or somewhere nearby. The list is updated monthly as BBS systems appear and disappear. The NGS BBS supports two telephone lines, you can call at 703-528-2612 or 703-528-8570. The file you need to download is GBBSxxxx.ZIP where the "xxxx" is equal to the year and month it was created. For instance, the update of the file created in August, 1995, would be GBBS9508.ZIP.

Also, many BBSs will maintain lists of other BBS systems in the same area. You may be able to dial into one BBS that doesn't carry genealogy information but does carry a list of the others in the area that do.

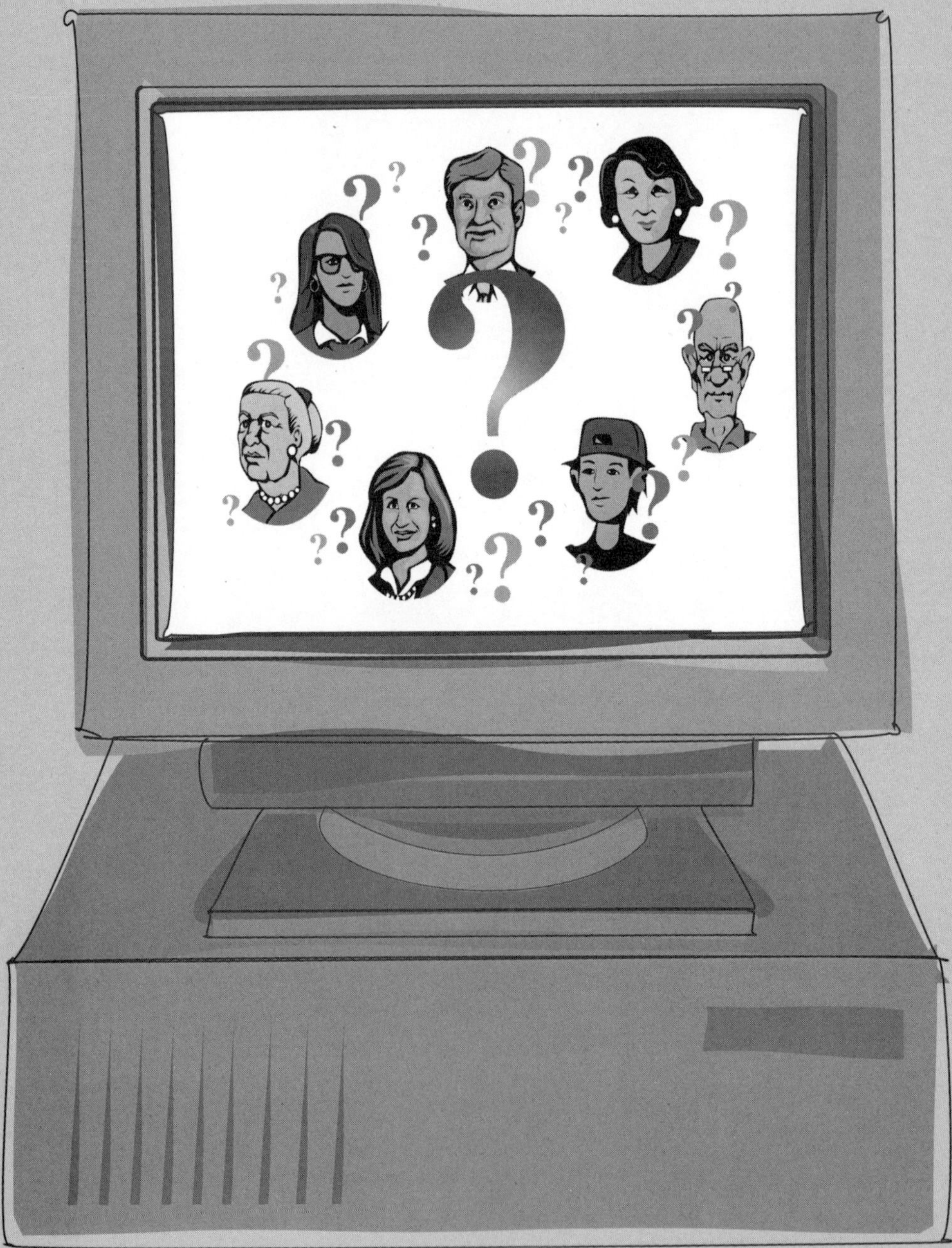

5

Taking *the* First **Steps:** Computerized **Genealogy** Research **Basics**

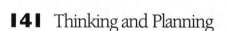

You've

decided to trace your family tree. Now what? Many people have asked the same question; some have gone no further. With the help of a computer and some simple guidelines, you can trace your own ancestry back many generations. You probably already know something about your family history. You know older relatives. Your parents and perhaps your grandparents have told you about their lives when they were young. Family recipes are prepared on special occasions. There may even be an old portrait or two up in the attic. You will want to base your genealogy search upon this known data first; it will be the foundation of your research.

Whatever your present knowledge, you can find a great deal more. Along the way you may encounter a few roadblocks or even a few detours into false information. But a little patience and persistence will pay off handsomely. All of this will be done in an orderly progression and this book will show you the methods to use. You will discover not only new names and new places, you will also learn a lot about the way history affected your family. You will learn why the family left the old country or why your ancestor moved to an unsettled wilderness. You will discover the impact of wars, droughts, or the hundreds of other things that affect people's lives. You may also learn more about yourself, especially the physical traits you inherited. Your height, the color of your eyes and hair, that gap between your teeth, and all the rest of your other physical attributes were obtained from your ancestors. If you had an ancestor who died at an early age of an inherited medical condition, you might want to know about that. It just might save your life!

For many people, the study of their ancestry progresses through three distinct stages; your search may be similar. If so, you will gain knowledge slowly at first. The knowledge you gain will initially be about your grandparents and maybe a generation or two earlier. You will learn not only their names and dates, but also the settings and events that shaped their lives. This will be a small number of people: four grandparents and perhaps all eight great-grandparents.

As you become experienced at finding records it will be easier to go back generation after generation. Now you will quickly pick up more and more ancestors—the number doubles at each generation. If you go back 300 years you may be researching more than 4,000 direct ancestors! While you may not obtain information about each and every one of them, it is often possible to identify

2,000 or more and to learn something about their lives. This will be the second stage of your genealogy research, that of gathering, sorting, and organizing information about thousands of individuals. At this point you will rely upon your computer extensively.

The third stage occurs when you have in fact found most of the readily available information about your ancestors. You have exhausted the secondary sources and now obtaining new information becomes more difficult. You may be surprised to learn that this is often the most enjoyable stage of all. You will have become the expert on the family tree and you will use your newly obtained detective skills to uncover bits and pieces of information overlooked by others. You may want to organize and print all of your research so that others may have the information too.

Thinking and Planning

You can easily start your genealogy research in "vacuum cleaner mode" in which you simply gather everything you can at random times and place it in one large pile. That actually is a good method of getting started, but after going back three or four generations the pile becomes large and unorganized. At that point you need to stop, organize, and then plan your further efforts. You will need to become skilled at detective work: There were two men that had the same name as your ancestor in that small village—which one is the correct one? How will you obtain the needed information to decide which was which?

You will need to organize your information. Traditionally, genealogists kept records called "family group sheets" in three-ring binders or similar information on 4 × 6-inch file cards. You will probably want to use a computer to simplify that work and to obtain reports easily. Still, you will need to decide which program you need and you will need to know which information to enter and how to enter it.

You will need to define your goals. Do you wish to focus only on your own family name? (Most people search all their ancestors, not just those of one last name.) Do you want to find all the descendants of a particular person? Defining your goals early will save you time and money in the long run. You will need to plan the search effort as well. You probably will not be able to travel to each and every place that your ancestors lived. How will you obtain records? You can normally obtain information without ever traveling yourself, but the details vary depending on where your ancestors lived. You need to plan your research in order to accomplish as much as possible without wasting time.

Of course, if you do have the luxury of traveling to the lands of your ancestors, by all means do so. Not only will you usually be able to find records there, the satisfaction of walking on the land that your ancestors walked upon is difficult to describe. It truly is the examination of your roots.

Along the way you will be pleasantly surprised by the helpful individuals you meet, even those you "meet" electronically. The clerk at a county courthouse may be overworked and very busy, but will still take the time to show you records. The people who help you on an electronic network may prove to be your strongest allies; they may have already done some of that work or similar work in that area and be willing to share their knowledge with you. Yes, there may be a few exceptions here and there, but most people involved in genealogy work enjoy helping others.

You will probably be surprised at the amount of information that you obtain. You may wish to preserve this information for others in the form of computer printouts or even a complete genealogy book. With or without a computer, such books become family heirlooms for generations.

Computers and Genealogy

The invention of the modern-day computer and computerized record keeping can be traced back to something near and dear to all genealogists: the United States Census. The 1880 census was conducted manually, as were all previous censuses. Tabulating the data and counting the population had become an almost impossible job. In 1887 the data from the census conducted seven years earlier still had not been fully compiled despite a large number of census workers involved in the task. The Census Office decided that the solution was in mechanizing the census process.

Bids were solicited from American inventors and industry for methods of simplifying the census collection and analysis. Herman Hollerith won the bid with his "tabulating machine" which used cards with holes punched in them to represent information. The 1890 census was conducted with the use of Hollerith's punched cards, and only six weeks later the Census Office was able to announce that the U.S. population was 62,622,250. The previous census had required seven years to determine the total population!

➜ *1890 Hollerith card reader*

Herman Hollerith founded his own company in Washington, D.C., and continued to work on and improve his tabulating machines. These mechanical monsters could quickly sort and filter information contained on punched cards. By the time Mr. Hollerith died in 1929, his company had gone public and had changed its name to the International Business Machine Corporation, or IBM for short.

IBM and many other computer companies continued to use punched cards until the early 1980s, nearly 100 years after their invention. The mechanized tabulating machines were replaced by electronic equivalents that could sort and organize faster and with less mechanical maintenance required. At long last, the punched card was replaced by other forms of data storage such as floppy disk, hard disk drives, and magnetic tape.

The Census Office, later renamed the U.S. Census Bureau, continues to be a big user of computers. In 1951 the Census Bureau used punched cards with UNIVAC I, one of the first of the modern electronic computers. Each census conducted since then has relied upon mainframe computers more than previous censuses.

Genealogists began to use these mainframe computers for their own purposes. The first use of a computer for personal genealogy apparently wasn't recorded, but it most likely was done by some employee who had access to his employer's multimillion dollar computer during evenings or weekends. The author of this book kept his genealogy data on 80-column punch cards in 1974 and used a Honeywell 200 mainframe computer to sort and print reports as needed. This computer weighed several thousand pounds, cost a quarter of a million dollars, and consumed enough electricity per hour to light the average household for a year.

The invention of the microcomputer quickly brought computing power to the individual. The first home computers appeared in 1977 with Radio Shack's TRS-80, Commodore's PET, and the Apple II from Apple Computing. Though primitive by today's standards, these computers did allow for limited use by genealogists. By 1982 the microcomputers were becoming powerful enough for serious use. In a survey published in the May 1982 issue of *Genealogical Computing* magazine, a survey of 125 computer-using genealogists revealed that the majority of them used a Radio Shack TRS-80 Model I or an Apple II computer, either one of which was equipped with two 5-1/4 inch floppy-disk drives, and an Epson dot-matrix printer. The average purchase price of these systems was reported to be $4,171.

Today, for a total purchase price of perhaps one-third that, the typical computer has many times the power and capacity of those used in 1982. Hard-disk drives of 500MB or more are common. The 8MB of memory that seems standard in today's systems is 500 times that of the typical 16 kilobytes of memory that was included in the TRS-80, and now it is available at a lower price to boot.

As you have already read, there is a wide variety of genealogy software available today to record the results of your genealogy research. If you already own a computer, it probably will suffice to get you started. You can obtain a genealogy program that matches your present computer's capabilities and use that for recording data. When you later "trade up" to a more powerful computer, you may wish to obtain a matching genealogy program that takes advantage of that power. You can simply export your data from the original program and then import it into the new program. Never, ever enter genealogy data into a program that doesn't support GEDCOM! You will want to move that data someday and all your efforts will be wasted if you have to type everything in a second time.

When shopping for a new computer, you may wonder, How long will it last? Reflect back upon the computers of 1982 listed earlier. Each of those systems represented the state of the art at the time they were purchased, and yet they seem so primitive just a few years later. But waiting until the prices drop is futile as well, as the prices continue to drop year after year. In short, it is impossible to wait until "the best time to buy a computer." You simply pick the time that is right for you, select the model that best suits your pocketbook, your present needs, and your projected needs. Take comfort in the fact that it will be much cheaper than the $4,000 computers of 1982.

When selecting a new computer, you will want to obtain one that supports the modern genealogy programs. Whether you purchase a Macintosh or a PC clone, a high-speed CPU and 8MB of memory are now within the reach of most people. You probably will want a disk drive with at least 300MB of storage capacity. Of course, a modem is a necessity for comparing notes with others online. Most modems sold today are 14,400 baud, but these will soon be replaced by units that operate at 28,800 baud. All the higher-speed modems will communicate just fine with modems of slower speeds.

CD-ROM drives are now common so the use of CD-ROM databases is much easier than just a few years ago. This has resulted in a quick growth in the number of CD-ROM genealogy discs available today. Purchasing all of these discs would be very expensive, but it is possible to rent them or to use them at various libraries. Besides, you will undoubtedly find other uses besides genealogy for the CD-ROM drive in your system.

A Word Processor or a Genealogy Program?

Many genealogists in the past have simply used their computers as word processors to record their information, and there's certainly nothing wrong with that. In fact, when the early genealogy programs first appeared on the market, they were so primitive that even the most diehard computer-oriented genealogists still used word processor text files to supplement their genealogy programs. They felt they had to record the sources of data, the biographical details, and the sometimes conflicting information that couldn't be squeezed into the database structure of the early programs. With today's powerhouse programs, the need for an external word processor to hold extra notes has just about disappeared.

Instead, the reverse has become true with a number of genealogy programs (Reunion, The Master Genealogist, Roots IV, Brothers Keeper, and so on): The word processor is now often used for output from the genealogy program. The more powerful genealogy programs are capable of keeping all the needed information that used to be relegated to a word processor. However, the data is exported from the genealogy program either in a word processor's native format or as a Rich Text Format (RTF) file that most leading word processors can import. The result can be polished-looking documents and even complete books.

The advantage of using a genealogy program instead of a word processor lies in the nature of databases: If you update a record in one place that information is automatically updated every time you use it later. For instance, if you find a corrected birth date for an ancestor and enter that into the genealogy program's database, every reference to that person will now automatically display the corrected information. In a traditional word processor, you would have to manually seek through the documents and replace every occurrence of that date. Of course, the chances of errors are much higher in a word processing document.

Much of the data entry in genealogy work is tedious at best. Using a proper genealogy program that is optimized for such data entry will greatly reduce the amount of time required for data entry, this allows you more time to search new records!

Finally, publishing one's work is probably the ultimate aim of most serious genealogists. This ensures that your hard work is preserved and made available to others, even future generations. Today's top-of-the-line genealogy programs allow for converting raw data, including full source notes, into "books" that are printed in a format that non-genealogists can read. Using a genealogy program for records management is easier than doing the same with a word processor. Adding new information and printing updated charts and books is also simplified. Best of all, the recording of your sources of information is easily converted to footnotes or endnotes by all the more powerful genealogy programs. Of course, the phrase "publishing one's work" doesn't mean large printed volumes in fancy bindings produced by the thousands. It can simply be a computer printout placed in a three-ring binder and shared with a few close family members. Whatever the audience or the number of copies produced, you will still want to create a work that you can be proud of!

6 *Gathering Information*

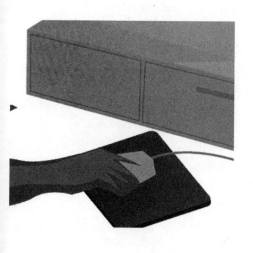

Creating
a record of one's ancestors is not a difficult task; you do not need to have an advanced degree in history or any other area of study. However, the recording of one's ancestors is much like the research done by scientists: The facts are the only things that count. You must concentrate on finding the facts and recording them, even when there is contradictory information. Once you have recorded the information, do not hesitate to go back and reexamine it when some new information is found that casts a different light on the original facts. The use of computers makes it easy to update and correct information entered weeks or even years earlier.

It is not enough to simply copy someone else's work, as that ensures that you will also copy that person's errors. The fact that something appears in print does not mean that it is accurate; many genealogy books have been printed with errors. In fact, probably no genealogy book is ever error-free.

In the excellent reference book *Genealogical Evidence: A Guide to the Standard of Proof Relating to Pedigrees, Ancestry, Heirship, and Family History*, Noel C. Stevenson writes "There are nearly 10,000 family histories and compilations in print and probably not more than 10 percent of them are worth the paper on which they are written. This is due solely to the fact that the worthless ones were compiled by persons who had no knowledge of the science of genealogy and particularly no comprehension of what constitutes proof. Anything they heard or saw from any source whatsoever was good enough."

The greater the separation in time and distance between the original event and the person who recorded it, the greater the chance of error. Using someone else's published information is an excellent method of quickly finding information, but you will need to examine both primary sources as well as secondary sources of genealogy information in order to verify accuracy.

Whenever you find contradictory information, record both sets of data. You may later find which one is believed to be more accurate. Until you are certain which is which, record both.

Start with Yourself

The time-honored method of researching your genealogy that always works best is to start with yourself. It is almost always impractical to quickly find some person of the right family name 100 or 200 years ago and then trace forward in time to yourself. The sheer logistics of dealing with all the people involved quickly becomes overwhelming. Success is almost always easier to obtain if you start with yourself, then enter the information about your two parents, followed by the information about your four grandparents, eight great-grandparents, and so on. You may be able to race through some family lines faster than others, but working backward in time is almost always the easiest and most effective plan.

Start with a family group sheet or sit in front of your computer with a genealogy program loaded. Enter your own name, date and place of birth, and your date and place of marriage if you are married. You probably will want to obtain a copy of your own birth certificate if you do not already have one. Then do the same for your parents. Next, enter the same information about any brothers and sisters you have. Now you have the data on one family.

Push back another generation and do the same thing for all four of your grandparents. Do you have any missing information? Most genealogy newcomers will. While not absolutely mandatory, it's best to enter data about your grandparents' other children, namely your aunts and uncles.

Never enter information that you *think* is correct, only enter what you know for a fact. However, it is permissible to enter data as *probable* data if you clearly label it as such. For instance, you might wish to enter a date as *circa 1924,* meaning approximately 1924, or you may wish to use a date of *before 1928* if you have sufficient proof of that. This is acceptable in situations where you know of one child who was born in 1928 and who had older brothers and sisters; you may not know the exact dates of birth for these older siblings but you are confident that they were born before 1928. Likewise, you can enter a location as *probably Bangor, Maine* in the location field. It's obvious that you do not have proof yet, it will be easy to locate this unverified information at a later time when you have more detailed records available.

Once you have completed as much as possible on your grandparents, you start to do the same with your great-grandparents. Most people will have a harder time doing this—the search is on!

Should you limit your research to only your own last name, or should you research all your ancestors? The choice is yours to make, but almost all genealogists want to find all their ancestors. You really are descended from thousands of different people, the overwhelming majority of them do not have the same last name as yours. Scientists who study DNA in the bloodstream will tell you that you inherit more genes from your mother than from your father. Likewise, your parents each inherited more genes from their mothers than from their fathers. You will want to pay special attention to this if you have family members who suffer from possibly inherited medical conditions, such as high blood pressure, obesity, some forms of cancer, diabetes, osteoarthritis, osteoporosis, glaucoma, cataracts, Huntington's Disease, asthma, and so on.

Limiting your search to only those who have the same last name as yours means that you will be ignoring the overwhelming majority of your ancestors and also ignoring your own medical and biological heritage.

Primary Sources versus Secondary Sources

Information written about a person during his or her lifetime or very shortly afterward by someone who had personal knowledge of the information is called a *primary source* or primary record of information. Primary sources are generally considered to be the most accurate, although they too may contain an occasional error. Primary sources include such things as a birth certificate, census records, a wedding certificate, an immigration record, an application for citizenship, a military discharge certificate, an application for a military pension, an obituary, a tax collector's records, and so forth. Each of these documents was written by the person involved or by someone who had personal knowledge of the information. Each of these documents was written at the time of the event and therefore can be trusted to almost always be accurate. There may be an occasional variation in name spellings or other minor errors, but the basic facts presented in such documents are usually correct, although exceptions do exist.

~🖥~

Information gathered and published some years after the original fact is called a *secondary source* and is generally considered to be less accurate. Most genealogy books written about specific families are considered to be secondary sources, as are history books, articles published in genealogy magazines, compiled lists of tombstones, and other such records.

As you start your genealogy searches you undoubtedly will rely heavily upon secondary sources. After all, if someone else has already done an excellent job of finding and publishing information, you certainly do not want to throw it away and start all over again. You merely use that information to simplify your work and to guide you in your efforts.

Several genealogy programs allow you to assign a "quality of data" value to the information recorded. This simply is your opinion of the reliability of this data. For instance, you might assign a numbering system of three to zero for each piece of information in your database:

3—Information obtained from a primary source with the data originally recorded by someone who had personal knowledge of the facts. An example of this would be a marriage record written by the minister who performed the ceremony.

2—Information obtained from a secondary source but believed to be generally accurate. An example of this might be the memoirs of someone writing about an individual he or she had known many years earlier.

1—Information obtained from a secondary source of unknown accuracy. An example of this might be a published book of "The Descendants of ...." written 200 years after the death of the first individual listed.

0—Information that is probably inaccurate. It may seem like a waste of time, but you really do need to record inaccurate data (but keep it separate from your main database). Frequently you will find something published that simply repeats something else published years earlier. If the first item was inaccurate, the second one will be also. In order to quickly identify data as erroneous you will need to keep track of the erroneous data you have already found, where you obtained it, and the reasons why you believe it to be inaccurate. By keeping track of information already proven false you can save yourself a lot of effort later!

It is not enough to copy from someone else's work, you need to discover the errors in their work as well.

Ancestors Were Human Too!

It is possible to simply record the name of each ancestor found, along with the place and date of birth, the place and date of marriage, and the place and date of death. In fact, many thousands of people have done just that: recorded only the most basic information. However, these people have missed out on their true family histories. Each of your ancestors was much more than a name and a few vital facts to be recorded in a computer database. Each person was an individual with feelings, hopes, desires, dreams, and a personality. Each person was affected by the people and events that surrounded them and they also had an effect on others. To truly know and understand your family's history, you need to collect biographical information whenever possible.

For instance, you may find that a particular ancestor was a 15-year-old bride who went on to have 10 children in 10 years and often was left alone with the children while her husband was at sea. Another may have failed at farming, gone through bankruptcy, and then loaded the family into a wagon and headed west in search of a new life. Still others may have had business or personal successes and failures, and you will find that a knowledge of this helps to understand who they were and why they did what they did.

One of my more interesting ancestors was Antoine Roy-Desjardins. He was originally recorded in my database with only his name and the date and place of death in Quebec Province. A few years later while scanning through Quebec court records of the late 1600s his name almost jumped off the page at me. He was listed as the murder victim at a particularly lurid murder story, having died at the hands of a jealous husband who returned home unexpectedly from a journey and found his wife and my ancestor in a rather indelicate situation. The date of the murder was indeed the same as the date of death that I had previously recorded in my database.

The outraged husband was then tried for murder, although he was found innocent "for reasonable cause." The record of the trial included a rather detailed description of the husband's absence, and his return home to find his wife in bed with her lover. Suddenly this ancestor became much more interesting than simply a name, date, and place! Had I only been collecting the basic data I would have missed one of the most interesting "family tree" stories in my family.

There are similar stories in almost everyone's family tree. You may find the ancestor's date of death is on the same day as an Indian attack on the village where he or she lived. You certainly will find stories of hardship and stories of good times. You may possibly find scandals or stories of good Samaritans.

Every family will have a wide variety of personalities in the family tree. There will be vagabonds and ne'er-do-wells along with others who are best described as "pillars of the community." Every family tree will contain a few illegitimate births, second marriages without benefit of a divorce from the first, and a variety of other social anomalies. These ancestors are to be valued, as they are truly humanized in your records. In the book *Researcher's Guide to American Genealogy*, Val D. Greenwood summed it up nicely: "If you are afraid of skeletons, then stay out of closets."

How to Take Notes

Even with the popularity of home computers, it's still easy to get lost in a sea of paper. You will be able to obtain data from computerized databases as described later in this book. However, much of your genealogy investigations will be based upon paper or microfilmed records or upon information published in various books. There are probably a thousand different methods of gathering the information from these records, and there is no one method that is best. You need to find a method that works for you and that you can use time and time again. I will describe a method that works well for me, but you may find better methods for your own use.

Taking a laptop computer along when visiting a library or a courthouse or a genealogy archive of some sort is a tremendous help. You can keep your entire database on a five-pound PC or Macintosh that slips into a briefcase or possibly into a large purse. Even the so-called "palmtop PC" can be valuable for carrying data for reference purposes. These shirt-pocket sized computers may store up to several megabytes of information, such as your entire genealogy database.

However, unless you are a high-speed touch typist you will quickly realize it is impractical to enter all the data into the computer while at the location of the records you are searching. The secret of research success is the liberal use of a photocopier and a large pad of paper. Between the two, you can quickly "vacuum up" a lot of information which you can then sort and organize after returning home. You can then transcribe as much or as little data as you wish into the computer. You may be collecting data in a hodgepodge manner, but the organizational capabilities of the home computer will sort and organize the information properly.

If you do not yet have the luxury of a laptop computer, simply print the information you already have about the families you expect to research on this trip to the library or archives. Having reference material on paper is almost as good as having it in the portable computer. If you wish, you may print family group sheets and pedigree charts on everyone in your database. Insert these into three-ring binders divided into appropriate sections. You might want to take notes directly on these forms. When you return home you can enter the newly obtained data into the computer and then print new replacement forms for your notebook.

Organize the Paper Trail

It's best to have a filing system for the data obtained. Most photocopies will be $8^1/_2 \times 11$ inches, so it's easiest to standardize on that same size for all paper notes. The consistent use of one size of paper makes things much simpler than the random collection of scraps of paper or old envelopes. You may want to start three-ring binders, one for each family name. If so, buy the pads of paper that already have the three holes punched. Another method is to use file folders. You can start with one folder per surname, and as you obtain more and more information you may want to divide the folders up by some other method. Do not throw the paper-based notes away after entering the data into the computer! You will occasionally need to go back and double-check your original notes.

When taking notes, I always write the family's surname in large letters across the top of each page and the current date in the top right corner. Immediately below the date I record the location of the data being searched, such as "Penobscot County Courthouse, Probate Records, 1832." That simplifies the filing system and also simplifies things if you need to go back and check anything again months later. In the case of photocopies, I do the same thing on the reverse side of the copy. Always use a pencil for this. Always use a new page for each new topic, such as each family or possibly for each person. Also, I always write in the top left of the paper a standard "code" for the person or the place and also the source of information.

How to Import Data from Available Databases

Computer technology has made it possible to obtain large amounts of genealogical information by downloading from an online system, by exchanging disks, or by copying computerized genealogy data from the CD-ROM at a local Family History Center onto a floppy disk. These files are normally in GEDCOM format and can be imported into almost any modern genealogy program.

However, you may already have a sizable computer database; simply importing someone else's data into yours could produce duplicate records and possibly inaccurate data if the other person's standards of genealogy research are not up to your own. You run the risk of trashing your own database by inserting hundreds or thousands of new records of unknown quality.

Instead, you need to first create a backup of your existing database for insurance purposes. Next, create a new database that is empty of all data and then import the newly obtained GEDCOM file into that. You can then use the power of your genealogy program to examine this new data. Once you are comfortable with this new data, you may want to copy part of it or possibly all of it into your main database. The exact instructions for doing all this will depend upon your choice of genealogy software, but all modern genealogy programs are capable of keeping two or more simultaneous databases that are isolated from each other.

Keep a Research Log

Keep a log of work that you have done and especially a log of work to be done in the future. Keeping accurate logs will reduce the chance of searching for the same data twice. Also, if you enter a genealogy library or archive of any sort carrying a list of specific tasks to be accomplished and records to be searched, you reduce the risk of being sidetracked and wasting time. Keeping a research log of future research to be accomplished is one of the secrets to maximizing your time.

A research log doesn't need to be fancy—that plain blue-lined white paper that you use for note taking will do just fine. However, the computer owner will probably want to keep the research log on the computer where it can be easily updated. A few genealogy programs, such as The Master Genealogist, keep research logs and task lists within the genealogy database.

You may want to keep a correspondence log if you do any letter writing. If making photocopies is not practical, keep a log of who you wrote to, the date the letter was sent, the topic of the letter, and the date a reply was received. Again, this log can be on paper or a simple text file on a computer.

Verbal Interviews

One of the greatest sources of information is tapped by interviewing older family members. Always take along pads of paper and several pencils. However, it's often best to also tape record the entire interview. Always ask permission first before recording. Take a rather small tape recorder, if possible, and once the record button has been pressed place the recorder out of direct sight of the person being interviewed. The person being interviewed may be a bit uncomfortable with the tape recorder at first, but that is usually swept aside as the memories start flowing.

The obvious advantage of taped interviews is that you can replay them later at your leisure and transcribe only the relevant information. Also, you may find information months or even years later that you want to have verified—the words on the tape that seemed unimportant at the time may become very important years later when new facts have been uncovered.

Some years ago I interviewed a 92-year-old great aunt who had an amazing memory. I recorded the entire two-hour conversation. Several years after her death I played the tapes again and discovered several pieces of information that hadn't seemed important at the time of our original conversation. Had I relied solely upon written notes her information would have been lost forever.

A hidden benefit of talking with older family members is that they often have photographs of your ancestors. The photographs may be long forgotten until a conversation starts about that person and then the person being interviewed suddenly recalls "Well, I think I've got his picture right here…." Without verbal interviews you might never know of family heirlooms like that.

An interview in person is always best, of course. However, that may not be possible. Invest in a long distance telephone call or two if necessary, and schedule it on a weekend when rates are low. You should call or write first to see if the person is agreeable to a telephone interview and have that person suggest the date and time. That way, he or she will be better prepared when you call. Telephone interviews can also be taped, but again always ask permission first.

If you are aware of any family scandals, approach them cautiously during the interview. The person being interviewed may not be comfortable talking about the subject. My own technique is to leave those topics until later in the interview. Once the people involved in the interview have become relaxed and comfortable with each other, detailed information is much more likely to be forthcoming.

Ask open questions, not leading ones. For instance, do not ask: "Your father was born in 1899, wasn't he?" Such information may be hard to recall at the moment and sometimes a Yes/No answer is not the best. You will usually obtain better results if you ask "Do you know where or when your father was born?" The ensuing conversation may meander a bit, but you do increase the odds of obtaining the information you want.

A skilled interviewer always prepares a checklist in advance. This checklist is a list of the topics to be discussed and the information that you wish to obtain.

Interviewing older family members can be a pleasure for both people. You should allow the conversation to roam a bit as that is when some of the best stories are revealed. However, during lulls in the conversation you should glance at your checklist to bring the topics back to the areas that you wish to pursue. In fact, if you think that perhaps you didn't get the full story on some piece of information, bring the topic up again later in the conversation. Something in subsequent discussions may have refreshed that memory and information missing earlier may be recalled in detail later in the conversation.

Old Photographs

Almost all genealogists also become collectors of old family photographs. Practically every family has old photo albums or a shoebox or two full of old pictures. Some of these may not be labeled or catalogued in any manner. The time to obtain information about them is now while knowledgeable family members are still alive. For instance, I found the picture shown on the next page in an unlabeled box of family pictures. I didn't realize at first that this was my father-in-law, whom I first met when he was in his fifties. He did not seem to me to resemble the child in the photograph. Also, until I saw this photo I did not realize that it was common to dress young boys in dresses for formal photographs in the early 1900s.

Other family heirloom photos may also surprise you. For instance, I discovered from the photo shown on page TK that there were triplets in the family. Both of these photos were faded after years of storage and have since been enhanced by a home computer equipped with a desktop scanner. Photo scanning and restoration are both discussed at length later in this book.

Analyze!

As you continually gather information you will want to analyze it and review it time and time again. One reason is to spot errors. Was the father really 75 years old when the child was born? Did these two brothers really have a 40-year age

→ *Wallace Carter Clayton*

This photograph was taken in 1911 and is an excellent example of the formal portraits of that time. It was common in many areas to dress young boys in dresses for formal pictures.

Arlene (Weeks) Clayton with triplet daughters

This photograph was faded and had a few blemishes. The contrast was enhanced electronically and the blemishes removed with PhotoStyler 2 software.

difference? And was that woman really married when she was 3 years old? Was this other person really born in Massachusetts in the 1500s? These and other errors are all published in numerous genealogy books.

Many genealogy programs have "sanity check" utilities. The wording and the exact method of operation will vary from one program to another. However, most of them will scan through the database looking for inconsistent or improbable entries. Most of these sanity checks examine dates and will report any that seem unlikely, such as a person with a marriage date only nine years later than the date of birth. No computerized sanity check is perfect, you will still need to watch for such inaccurate information yourself.

Backups, Backups, Backups

Who hasn't had a case of accidentally erasing a file? Accidents do happen. There may be cases of hardware or software failure in your computer that will erase or corrupt your database. If you spend many hours of work recording your family's history, you do not want it knocked out in a few milliseconds by some computer glitch. Sometimes things other than simple computer problems can destroy all your work.

One of the sad pictures seen on national television a few years ago was a woman in southern California standing in front of her home that was burning in one of the large brush fires. When the television reporter asked about her losses, her first answer was that she had just lost 20-years worth of work researching her family tree as all her records were in one filing cabinet in the house.

A happier ending occurred on CompuServe's Genealogy Forum where one person uploaded a GEDCOM-format copy of his entire genealogy database to CompuServe so that someone else could obtain a copy of it and make comparisons. The first person later had a computer failure that destroyed his hard drive and he had no backups. However, after obtaining a new hard drive he was able to retrieve a copy of his own database from CompuServe and thereby restore it completely to his new drive.

You should always keep one copy of your database at another location. On the same evening that you sit down to pay your monthly bills, perhaps you should copy your genealogy database (and your computerized checkbook!) to floppy disks and take them to work with you the next day. Leave the copies at work for one month. Or give them to a neighbor or friend for safekeeping.

Make Your Information Available to Others

As you gather genealogy information you should plan on making that data available to others. Both future generations within your own family and other genealogy researchers who may be distant relatives will want your data. Your hard work should be made available to others.

The traditional method of doing this has been to print genealogy books and that tradition is expected to continue for a number of years yet. Conduct all your research now as if you plan to publish a book someday. That may actually happen!

Computerized databases have recently become available and you may wish to contribute your data to those databases. The data stored in these databases will be available to millions of people in electronic format, which will be much easier to use and also much cheaper than printed volumes. The way to use these electronic databases will be covered later in this book.

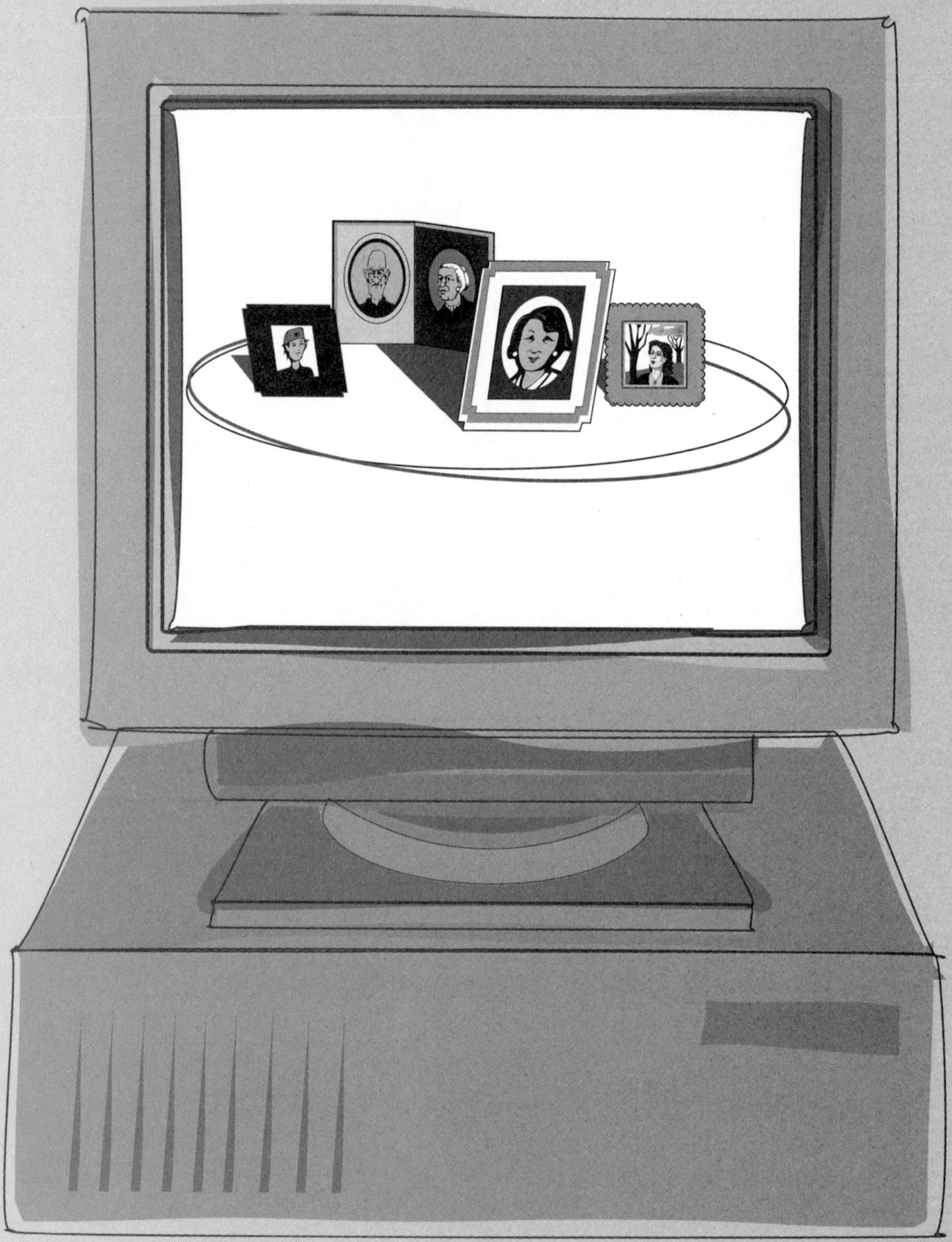

7 | *Computerized Photography*

Compiling

information about your ancestry doesn't need to be limited to the simple collection of facts as text; you can also gather photographs from the late 1800s right up to the present. These can easily be incorporated into your genealogy database and made available for retrieval whenever you wish. Scanned photographs can be added to printouts and can even be included in the books that many genealogy programs will produce.

Perhaps one of the most satisfying uses of your computer is for the restoration and enhancement of old family heirloom photographs. If you have a faded or darkened picture of your great-grandfather in a Civil War uniform, you can scan the photograph and then use digital tools to add contrast to the photo or to darken it as needed. Using modern graphics software you can delete scratches and blemishes from old photographs. It's possible to even touch up the ancestor's image a bit, to remove a blemish or birthmark that shows in the original photograph.

In one extreme case that I saw recently, a modern family portrait had been digitally altered to remove an unwanted brother-in-law from the photo entirely! Since he was no longer considered to be a family member after the divorce, his image was removed from a group picture and the space where he had been standing was filled in with a bit of background from a second photograph taken at the same location on the same day but showing different people. The new photographs were then reproduced on a high-quality printer designed for photography professionals and copies were distributed to family members. All of this was done by a digital "cut-and-paste" effect. The photograph that resulted appeared to be an original and no one needs to be the wiser. All of the work was done on a home computer except that the final output was sent on floppy disk to a professional service for printing.

Photographs are converted to binary images by a device called a *scanner* and are then stored in a computer in the same manner as any other file. There are many scanners available today and prices and quality vary widely. On the low-end of the scale, *handheld scanners* are available in the $100 to $300 price range. Moving up in quality, black-and-white desktop scanners are available for around $300 to $600. These are referred to as *flatbed scanners*, as a photograph of 8 × 10 inches or even larger can be placed upon its flat surface and scanned. Color flatbed scanners are more costly. Color units will cost $600 to $1,200 for the typical home computer. Moving even further up the price scale you can find the professional-quality units that are normally found only in printing businesses or in the hands of other professional users.

Scan It Yourself?

Commercial scanning operations will scan your photographs for you and make them available on floppy disk or even on a CD-ROM disc called *PhotoCD*. A single scan at a local service bureau may cost $10 per picture, while a roll of film may be transferred to a PhotoCD for a cost of $30 per roll or so. However, if you rely upon someone else to do the scanning for you then you are limited by the quality of the equipment used as well as the skill level and the personal attention supplied by the person operating the scanning equipment. In order to obtain optimum pictures, it may be necessary to scan the original several times making incremental adjustments between each scan. You may be able to rent time on a scanner for $35 per hour or so and do the work yourself. However, if you are going to do much scanning, it quickly becomes cost-effective to purchase your own scanner and spend as much time as you like refining the photographs. You will certainly save time and you probably will save money as well. The greatest satisfaction, however, is that you gain control over your own work. As you gain expertise and experience, you will learn how to make tone corrections and to enhance your photographs in a manner that meets your needs.

Handheld Scanners versus Flatbed Scanners

You may be tempted to purchase one of the handheld scanners that are advertised for $200 or less. These low-cost units are capable of scanning photographs as wide as 4 inches or so and some may include software that allows you to scan larger photographs in two or more passes and then electronically "paste" the picture back together with your computer. However, use of a handheld scanner requires a great deal or patience and manual dexterity. You must scan in a straight line and at a steady speed. Pasting pictures together is tedious at best even on the highest quality scans. It becomes very frustrating when the two sections do not line up just right, a situation that happens frequently.

Using a handheld scanner sounds easy when reading the advertisements, but many of these scanners are now gathering dust as the owners gave up trying to do serious work with them. If you are serious about scanning you will want to obtain a flatbed scanner that is at least large enough to scan a standard 8.5 × 11-inch document in one pass. If your only purpose is to scan old family photographs that are black-and-white prints, then an appropriate flatbed scanner won't cost much more than a handheld unit. However, most people want to use the scanner for many things besides old photographs, so color scanners are much more popular. Most color scanners sold today are in the $600 to $1,000 price range. Always look for the software that is included with the scanner, if any. Several of the more expensive scanners include bundled software that would cost several hundred dollars if purchased separately. That reduces the effective cost of the purchase for many people.

Scanning and Graphics Software

Scanners work by breaking the image into tiny dots, called *pixels*. Each pixel represents one tiny spot on the original photograph or drawing, and that pixel is then represented as a colored dot within the computer's memory or as stored on disk. A complete picture consists of many thousands of pixels. When viewed by the human eye, these pixels are not visible individually. Instead, they blend together in what appears to be a true photograph or drawing. This is true whether viewed on the computer's screen or printed on paper.

Scanners typically will separate the picture being scanned into 75 to 400 dots (pixels) per inch. Some of the more expensive scanners go as high as 2,400 dots per inch. When reproduced on screen, normal resolution of 75 to perhaps 150 pixels per inch as used in Super VGA monitors typically display 1,024 pixels horizontally and 768 pixels vertically. Therefore, a 6 × 5-inch image scanned at 150 pixels per inch will almost fill the screen. Modern laser printers are capable of printing 300 to 400 dots per inch. To retain a photograph's normal size it should be scanned at the same resolution as the intended printer is capable of delivering.

You may find two resolutions quoted in a scanner's specifications: optical resolution (sometimes call real resolution) and interpolated resolution. The *optical resolution* is what the scanner's hardware is capable of producing. *Interpolated resolution* is what the included software can do to enhance the image even more. Interpolated resolutions are typically double or quadruple the optical resolution. This happens when the software generates new pixels in between scanned pixels and colors them in a "best guess" fashion based upon the actual colors and shading of adjacent scanned pixels. Again, the quality of software varies widely. Higher-priced software actually can add to a scanner's output but some other interpolation programs actually detract from the scanned image. When evaluating scanners pay attention to the optical resolution. Interpolated resolution is not as important.

What scanning resolution do you need? If you want to use scanned photographs in laser-quality printouts, purchase a scanner that is capable of at least 300 pixels per inch, although 400 pixels per inch is even better. Scanners that only offer lower resolution are available cheaply now as manufacturers clear out their inventories, but anyone who is interested in scanning photographs will not want one.

When reading advertisements for scanners you may get the impression that the best way to compare the quality of scanners is to simply compare the maximum resolution they are capable of producing. This insinuation is often found in advertisements of cheaper scanners that claim to have better capabilities than more expensive units. However, the resolution (pixels per inch) is only one measure of a scanner's capability and can be misleading if considered alone. The number of pixels has very little to do with the overall quality of a scanned image. Theoretically a scanner that is capable of more pixels per inch should produce a more detailed picture. However, it says nothing about color tone reproductions, contrast and clarity, speed, color casting, interpolation, or moiré patterns. A cheap scanner with high resolution may never produce images that you want to use in your genealogy work. If you are not familiar with scanning, ask to see some photographs scanned by the model of scanner that you are contemplating purchasing. Compare it to scanned photos from competitive units.

Many scanners include bundled software that has a purchase price of $200 or even as high as $600. If you have a need for such software, carefully check what is already included with the scanner. A scanner that costs $200 more but includes $600 worth of free software that you will eventually purchase anyway may be the better bargain. Most scanners include either Photoshop or Photo-Styler, two of the leading programs in scanned image manipulation and enhancement software. You will frequently find *OCR* (optical character recognition) software included, such as WordScan or OmniPage. These programs convert scanned images of text pages and convert them into text files. This will be described in detail later in this book.

If you wish to purchase additional software for other purposes, make sure that the scanner supports the *TWAIN* standard. TWAIN allows any compatible software to use that scanner. Most scanning software supports TWAIN and therefore will work with any TWAIN-compliant hardware.

Scanned graphics files are available in many formats including an alphabet-soup collection of file standards. These standards include: TIFF, GIF, JPEG, BMP, PCX, WMF, and many others. Each one is capable of storing graphics, so why the many standards? One answer is that some of the more modern formats can store picture information in smaller (compressed) files. Scanned images can become very large—a 1 × 1-inch photograph scanned at 300 dots per inch contains 90,000 pixels (300 vertically times 300 horizontally). An 8 × 10-inch photograph scanned at 300 dots per inch contains more than 7 million pixels. This may require a large amount of disk space to store that one picture.

The original PCX format or PC Paintbrush software may require 7 megabytes of disk space to store that high resolution scanned image of an 8 × 10-inch color photograph. Tagged image file format (*TIFF*) files allow for a more faithful reproduction of color than the older file formats. TIFF also has the advantage of being cross-platform compatible as TIFF files are commonly used on both Macintosh and Windows computers. TIFF also includes some file compression that results in less disk space being used for storage.

Encapsulated PostScript (*EPS*) files are common in commercial printshops. PostScript is a "printer language" and an Encapsulated PostScript file can be printed on any PostScript-compatible printer without significant change in printer size, color, or resolution. The other file formats are not as universal. EPS files do consume more disk space than most other formats, however. Also, most graphics programs cannot read EPS files; it is more commonly used for output only.

Graphics Interchange Format (*GIF*) was invented by CompuServe for use in online systems but now has become popular elsewhere. GIF includes a method of compressing files in a manner that often results in a disk file that is only 25 to 35 percent the size of the original. This is done with no loss in clarity or resolution. GIF is very popular when graphics files are to be sent over telephone lines, as the smaller sizes result in faster file transfers and reduced online charges.

A new format is *JPEG* (Joint Photographic Experts Group) which includes even more compression than the other file formats. In fact, when storing JPEG files most software will allow you to specify the amount of compression to be used. The drawback to JPEG is that there is always a tradeoff of compression versus image quality—the more the compression, the greater the resolution loss. However, modest amounts of file compression results in small losses that are not noticeable to the human eye. Higher compression levels may not be suitable, however. JPEG is becoming popular for use in full-motion computer graphics, as the smaller files can be quickly read from disk and then displayed on screen as a series of "frames" in a movie.

Graphics Printing

Displaying a scanned image on a computer screen almost always results in an excellent picture. Modern computer monitors are capable of displaying thousands of colors and an almost infinite amount of shading. The limiting factor in on-screen displays is the video board within the computer. Printer technology, however, has not advanced as far. No printer found in a hobbyist's home can approach the clarity of an original photograph. Photographic-quality printers do exist but prices are typically $100,000 or so. The normal laser and inkjet printers found in homes will not approach that level of detail.

For scanned black-and-white photographs, a laser printout may be acceptable for hobbyist use. Color scanned images can be converted to grayscale by the software used and these too will result in passable printouts. Moving into color may not be as satisfying, however. Modern color inkjet printers work well on drawings but normally lack the shading and color variations needed for photographs.

Most genealogists use scanners for onscreen displays and for "quick print-outs" of black-and-white photographs. For more serious work they leave a blank spot on their printouts and then have a professional print shop add in photographs when printing multiple copies of a document.

Photo Restorations and Enhancements

The actual mechanics of doing the scanning and enhancements of old photographs requires only three things: patience, patience, and still more patience. Of course, an artistic eye will also help a great deal. You may find yourself scanning the same photograph over and over, changing the settings in your software just a bit in between each scan. Once you have gotten the image that is "just right" you save it on disk and then the real work begins. You will need to remove scratches, reduce or increase contrast, and otherwise work on the photograph in microscopic detail. While this may be tedious, the end result is often far better than what is typically done in a photo lab and it is produced at a far lower cost besides.

Image manipulation software such as Photoshop or PhotoStyler allows you to "blow up" a picture onscreen until it is many times larger than the original. You can see every pixel clearly. You then use the program's "paint brush" features to move around the image and to change the image pixel by pixel. You can also use the program's built-in features to enhance contrast and to change shading in parts of the image. This will be much faster than changing one pixel at a time. You can "cut and paste" entire sections of a photograph for more drastic changes to an original photograph. The figures on the next two pages show a restoration of an heirloom photograph; while this particular restoration was done by an experienced professional photographer, the hardware and software that she used is typical of that found on home computer systems. You can do the same kind of restorations on your computer.

Once you are satisfied with the work, you save the image again to disk in its normal size. If the picture is an especially valuable heirloom, you'll probably want to have it professionally printed. Photo businesses (service bureaus) will accept scanned images on floppy disks and print them on photographic-quality printers for a modest fee.

An Unaltered Heirloom Photograph

This is a photograph as originally inherited by Gay Spencer, one of the forum managers on CompuServe's Genealogy Forum and a professional photographer. The original tintype had darkened so much over the years that the image was barely visible.

Removing scratches is tedious. Take care not to induce any scratches into the original scanned image. This obviously is not always possible on old photographs but you should always handle any photo as if it were priceless. Many microscopic scratches are created by mishandling a dusty photograph. When a dusty photograph is placed in an envelope or rubbed against any other surface, the dust creates minute scratches. Fingerprints on a print are far worse; one fingerprint may require hours of work to remove. There are chemicals that can help undo minor damage to a photograph, but if improperly used they easily result in

The Digitally Restored Photograph

Spencer scanned the photo at the highest resolution possible in order to enlarge the image as much as possible. Then, she used several commodity programs to lighten the scanned image and to enhance the contrast.

even greater damage. Consult a professional photographer before applying any chemicals to a valuable photograph. Always keep all photographs as dust-free and uncontaminated as possible.

Optical Character Recognition

Converting out-of-print books and other valuable genealogy sources is an excellent use of scanners. There are tens of thousands of books printed about different families' ancestry. Most of these books are limited editions printed by small companies that may not even be in business today. Even the best-equipped genealogy libraries only have a small percentage of all these books on their shelves. Also, many of these books are poorly indexed. While there may be information about your ancestors available in print, finding those books is a difficult task.

Today's technology is changing all that thanks to *OCR* scanning. *Optical character recognition* is the process of converting scanned documents into text that you can edit and then print with a word processor or even a genealogy program. Each page is scanned on a flatbed scanner and the "picture" is stored on disk in the same manner as any other scanned image. Then the OCR software analyzes all the pixels within that picture to find and identify individual letters and words. Each letter is then stored in a different file as regular text which can later be imported into any word processor program and edited as desired.

Once the book is in text format many software tools can be used. Whether a regular word processor or specialized text retrieval software is used, it is now possible to quickly find anyone by name whether they are listed in the index or not. The computer will search the entire file and find the name within seconds. Indexing software can be used to find every occurrence of any word in the entire book.

When scanning photographs you only are concerned about one sheet of paper at a time. You place that sheet upon the scanner and scan it, you then work on the image. When scanning books that may have hundreds of pages, such a method is tedious. A common accessory to most flatbed scanners is an automatic document feeder, or *ADF* for short. These function in much the same manner as the paper feed on an office copier. You place 50 or more pages into the ADF, click the mouse a few times in your software and then you can walk away. The ADF inserts one page at a time into the scanner and the OCR software scans that one page. When completed, that page is ejected, a new page automatically is inserted and the process continues. Most OCR software will allow you first scan all the odd-numbered pages. Once completed, you turn the stack of pages over, reinsert them, and then the OCR software scans the even-numbered pages (in reverse order). Once completed, the OCR software determines the correct order and merges all the pages together accordingly. The obvious drawback is that you do need to cut the binding off the book, something you may not wish to do to a 100-year old genealogy book. An ADF typically adds $300 to $500 to the purchase price of a scanner.

OCR scanning is still an inexact science despite major advances in the past few years. It is indeed rare to have a page scanned and OCR converted that is entirely error-free. The OCR software uses "artificial intelligence" techniques to analyze each part of the image that appears to be text and then determine the most likely character in each location. On clear black text printed in a modern font on white paper the accuracy may reach 99.8 percent. On older books with irregular fonts, faded ink, and paper that has become gray with age, accuracy quickly drops off. Also, any book that is a photocopy of the original will normally create many more errors in the scanning process than an original document.

For instance, the figure on page 180 shows a page from a typical older genealogy book. In this case, the book is a photoreproduction of the *History and Genealogy of the Eastman Family of America* by Guy S. Rix, printed in 1901 by the Press of Ira C. Evans, Concord, NH, and scanned more than 90 years later on a Hewlett-Packard ScanJet IIcx.

This photo reproduction looks good to the human eye but the OCR software struggles with it. Here's the output from WordScan Plus 3.0 OCR software before human interaction:

8   EASTMAN FAMILY OF AMERICA.
Roger Eastman came from Langford, county of Wilts, and
sailed from Southampton in April, i638, in the ship Confidence, John jobson, master, bound for Massachusetts Bay
Colony.

On the ship's papers he was entered as a servant of John Saunders. It is believed that on account of the emigration laws, or for political reasons, his real rank was higher than' appears. Many traditions have been handed down, but it is believed that Roger Eastman was the sole ancestor of all the Eastmans in this country. The name has been, in some cases, spelled 11 Easman," even by members of the same family. No record of his marriage has been found or of his wffe's full name, and ft is only by tradition that we suppose ft to be 11 Smith." Roger Eastman received lands in the first division in Salisbury, in i640-3. His minister's tax in **i65o** was 8s. 3d.

From Salisbury the tribe dispersed, but the major part settled in the southern towns of New Hampshire and the northern towns ot'Massachusetts.

The third generation, however, settled farther north, following up the Merrimack river, while others settled further south in Massachusetts and Connecticut and cthers in Maine. From these places they scattered over the Unfted States and Canada.

CHILDREN.

12.**i. John2** b. Jan. 9, **1640.**
3. ii. Nathaniel2, b. March 18,1643.
4. iii. Philip2, b. Oct. 20, 1644.
5. iv. **Thomas2,** b. Sept. 11, 1646.
.6. v. Timothy3, b. Sept. 29, 1648.
7. vi. Joseph2, b. Nov. 8, 1650.
8. vii. Benjamin2, b. Dec. 12,1632.
9. viii. **Sar@h2,** b. July 25, 1655.
'I@o. **ix. S&M)*12,** b. Sept. 20, 1657.
ii. X. Riih7 b. Jan. 21, 1661.

You will notice several common scanning problems in the above text. The number "one" is easily confused with lower-case letter I; the year 1638 became i638. In another instance an "i" was translated as "f" making "wffe" instead of "wife," and now we live in the "Unfted States." Uppercase and lowercase are not always translated properly, especially when the two letters resemble each other closely. The name "John Jobson" became "John jobson." WordScan Plus did an excellent job on the children's names that were printed in a tiny font on the original text. However, one critical error was created on the listing for the child Benjamin in the above list. The original book lists his date of birth as Dec. 12, 1652,

A Photoreproduction of a Page from an Older Genealogy Book

8   EASTMAN FAMILY OF AMERICA.

Roger Eastman came from Langford, county of Wilts, and sailed from Southampton in April, 1638, in the ship Confidence, John Jobson, master, bound for Massachusetts Bay Colony.

On the ship's papers he was entered as a servant of John Saunders. It is believed that on account of the emigration laws, or for political reasons, his real rank was higher than appears.

Many traditions have been handed down, but it is believed that Roger Eastman was the sole ancestor of all the Eastmans in this country. The name has been, in some cases, spelled " Easman," even by members of the same family. No record of his marriage has been found or of his wife's full name, and it is only by tradition that we suppose it to be " Smith." Roger Eastman received lands in the first division in Salisbury, in 1640–3. His minister's tax in 1650 was 8s. 3d.

From Salisbury the tribe dispersed, but the major part settled in the southern towns of New Hampshire and the northern towns of Massachusetts.

The third generation, however, settled farther north, following up the Merrimack river, while others settled further south in Massachusetts and Connecticut and others in Maine. From these places they scattered over the United States and Canada.

CHILDREN.

2.   i.   John[2], b. Jan. 9, 1640.
3.   ii.   Nathaniel[2], b. March 18, 1643.
4.   iii.   Philip[2], b. Oct. 20, 1644.
5.   iv.   Thomas[2], b. Sept. 11, 1646.
6.   v.   Timothy[2], b. Sept. 29, 1648.
7.   vi.   Joseph[2], b. Nov. 8, 1650.
8.   vii.   Benjamin[2], b. Dec. 12, 1652.
9.   viii.   Sarah[2], b. July 25, 1655.
10.   ix.   Samuel[2], b. Sept. 20, 1657.
11.   x.   Ruth[2], b. Jan. 21, 1661.

but the OCR software stumbled on the number 5 and said that the year was 1632. Such a difference in dates is critical in genealogy work.

A minute or two of manual work is required on this page to clean up the errors. The word processor's spell checker helps a lot, of course, but will not help much in all the names, dates, and places common to genealogy books. A spell checker will never find the 20-year error in Benjamin's date of birth. Still, even with the manual interaction required, OCR scanning of old books is usually much faster than retyping everything!

One or two commercial companies have started OCR scanning of old genealogy books and releasing them on CD-ROM discs. Profit margins are thin when producing scanned books of individual family names; these companies have mostly reproduced standard "genealogy classics" such as the major books of immigrants or other documents that appeal to thousands of genealogists. Only a few family surname books have been scanned as there is less demand for those volumes. If you have such a book and would like to have it made available to others, you can scan it yourself. As it is a "labor of love," you will not be concerned about profits. You can distribute the book to others on floppy disks, by uploading it to online systems, or by donating it to a CD-ROM manufacturer. Your efforts will benefit future genealogists for many years.

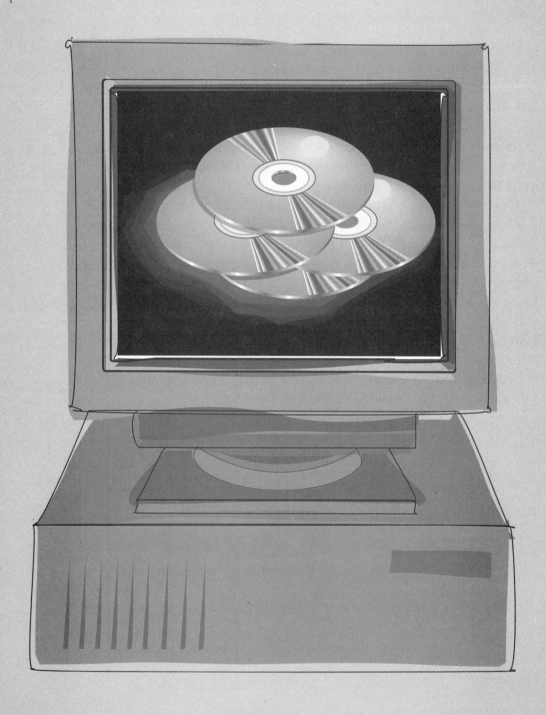

8 CD-ROM and Photo CD

Most desktop computers sold today include a CD-ROM drive. These drives will read the small, removable plastic CD-ROM discs that are available by the hundreds in any well-equipped computer store. The CD-ROM discs on the market today include hundreds of games as well as encyclopedias, reference manuals, pictures, and many other applications.

The CD-ROM is unmatched in its storage capacity. One disc can store up to 650MB of data—that is roughly the equivalent of 100 printed volumes of text. The abbreviation "CD-ROM" stands for "Compact Disc—Read Only Memory." The CD-ROM discs are similar to the popular audio CD discs: They are 4.71 inches in diameter (12 cm) and weig about one-half ounce. Regular CD-ROM discs are made of plastic with an aluminum coating on one side. The cost of the materials in one CD-ROM disc is about one cent. The cost of acquiring the data, converting it to CD-ROM format, packaging, advertising, and so on accounts for the purchase price.

The low cost of replicating CD-ROM discs makes it ideal for many applications, including genealogy. It is possible to produce and distribute large volumes of genealogy data at very low cost. Also, by using the search and indexing capabilities of computer software you can quickly scan through these databases looking for specific information. You can quickly find data on a CD-ROM disc that might remain undiscovered in a printed version of the same information.

The compact disc was created and defined in a series of proprietary standards by a joint effort of Sony and Philips. Compact disc-audio was introduced as a commercial product in 1982. The first CD-ROM computer applications were introduced for sale in late 1985, with the first genealogy database released on CD-ROM disc by Automated Archives, Inc. in 1990.

Data is "burnt" onto the plastic disc by the manufacturer. Your CD-ROM disc drive uses a tiny laser to shine on the CD-ROM disc and the data is retrieved from the reflections captured by a photocell. CD-ROM data is recorded in pits; there are 2.8 billion pits on a typical CD-ROM. As a point of reference, if each pit were the size of a grain of rice, the diameter of one CD-ROM disc would be longer than four football fields. Data is recorded in one spiral track, much like a phonograph record. These tracks are 1.6 millionth of a meter (roughly 60 millionths of an inch) apart.

The last three letters in CD-ROM stand for "read only memory" as these discs cannot be written to once created at the factory. Writeable CD discs are just appearing in the marketplace now although prices have not yet fallen to the point where a genealogy hobbyist will use them. There are other types of optical discs called WORM (Write Once, Read Many) that are writeable, but these are not used for distributing genealogy databases. WORM discs are not compatible with CD-ROM discs.

CD-ROM disc drives operate much more quickly than floppy-disk drives but are much slower than regular hard drives. Newer CD-ROM drives are double speed while some of the more expensive units are triple speed and quadruple speed. This refers to the speed in reading data compared to the original CD-ROM drives. Speed can be critical in multimedia applications but is generally not as important when using genealogy CD-ROM discs. The genealogy discs that are available for sale today are not multimedia. A faster drive will allow for faster database searches of course, but there is no critical requirement to use the higher-speed and higher-priced drives.

One of the major advantages of a CD-ROM disc is that there is no degradation of data caused by constant use. Data is read by a laser light; no mechanical contact is made. Data lasts essentially forever on a CD-ROM disc whereas it eventually becomes unusable on a frequently used floppy disk. Another advantage is that the CD-ROM disc is unaffected by magnetic fields. Unlike floppy disks, CD-ROM discs may be stored near magnets, electric motors, and power transformers. Finally, CD-ROM discs have a very long lifetime. While nobody yet knows what the typical life expectancy of a CD-ROM disc is, the discs available today will probably outlive the owners. CD-ROM discs are expected to last at least one human lifetime.

However, these discs are not totally impervious. They don't like to be abused, exposed to temperature extremes or excess humidity. Also, most CD-ROM discs are sensitive to high-intensity ultraviolet light. Always pick up a CD-ROM disc by its edges and never allow fingerprints on the disk surface itself. These are *optical* discs: any smudges, fingerprints, or minute scratches can cause damage to the data stored on the disc.

You probably will not use a CD-ROM drive exclusively for genealogy. You may want to have a double-speed or triple-speed drive in order to use the many multimedia discs that are available. Any of these CD-ROM drives will work with any of today's genealogy discs.

Genealogy CD-ROM Discs

One major producer of genealogy CD-ROM discs is the Church of Jesus Christ of Latter-day Saints. They produce CD-ROM discs of their genealogy databases for use in their Family History Centers located around the world. These discs are not yet available for purchase by private individuals. However, you can use them at no cost by visiting a local Family History Center near you. All of this is explained in detail in Chapter 9.

The largest producer of CD-ROM discs for sale to the general public is Automated Archives, Inc., a division of Banner Blue Software. They produce a large list of CD-ROM discs, many of which are also distributed by other companies. A partial list of their CD-ROM discs includes

- Marriage records indexes for selected states, 1624-1981
- Social Security death benefits records, 1937-1993
- United States census indexes for many states, 1634-1880
- Ireland census indexes for selected counties, 1831 & 1841
- Automated family pedigrees, 1500-1992
- Various mortality and miscellaneous state records indexes, 1685-1992
- Selected state land records, 1700-1908
- Military records for U.S. volunteer soldiers, 1784-1811
- Family history collection with the complete text of 217 genealogy research books

These discs may be purchased directly from Automated Archives or from any of a number of distributors. Depending upon how much the distributors will discount from list price, the price on each of these CD-ROM discs varies from about $20 each to about $75 each. Not all of the U.S. censuses have been indexed yet. The list of available CD-ROM discs includes

Pre-1790 Colonial America	From miscellaneous censuses taken in the Colonies
1790 United States	About 580,000 head of household
1800 Great Lakes, Mid-Atlantic, South	About 760,000 head of household
1800 New England, NY	About 440,000 head of household
1810 Great Lakes, Mid-Atlantic, South	About 700,000 head of household
1810 New England, NY	About 700,000 head of household
1820 Great Lakes, Mid-Atlantic, South	About 900,000 head of household
1820 North Eastern States	About 600,000 head of household
1830 Great Lakes, Mid-Atlantic, South	About 650,000 head of household
1830 North Eastern States	About 600,000 head of household
1840 Great Lakes, Mid-West	About 700,000 head of household
1840 Mid-Atlantic	About 700,000 head of household
1840 New England, NY	About 700,000 head of household
1840 South	About 700,000 head of household
1850 DC, MD, NC, VA, WV	About 800,000 head of household
1850 IL, IA, MI, MN, MO, WI	About 900,000 head of household
1850 KY, TN	About 800,000 head of household

1850 Mid-Atlantic	About 800,000 head of household
1850 New England	About 700,000 head of household
1850 New York	About 1,200,000 head of household
1850 Ohio & Indiana	About 900,000 head of household
1850 Southern states	About 900,000 head of household
1860 AL, AR, FL, GA, LA, SC	About 1,000,000 head of household
1860 Connecticut	Head of household
1860 DC, MD, NC, VA, WV	About 1,000,000 head of household
1860 DE, NJ, PA	About 1,000,000 head of household
1860 IL, IN	About 800,000 head of household
1860 Maine	Head of household
1860 Massachusetts	Head of household
1860 New York	About 1,200,000 head of household
1860 Vermont	Head of household
1860 Wisconsin	Head of household
1870 Chicago, St. Louis & Baltimore	Head of household
1870 KY, NC, VA, WV	Head of household
1870 North & South Carolina	Head of household
1870 Pennsylvania Western Counties	Head of household
1870 Virginia & West Virginia	Head of household
1880 Cook Co., IL	Head of household
1880 OH. (OH. Gen. Soc. CD)	About 800,000 head of household

In addition, a CD-ROM disc of the 1831 and 1841 Ireland censuses is available.

New titles are being added daily. Contact Banner Blue directly for an updated list. All of the census CD-ROMs contain *indexes* only, not full transcripts of the original records. These indexes will contain a person's name and a code that references the page in the original census where he or she was recorded (*enumerated*). You will then need to look at a microfilm copy of the original census record to obtain the detailed information.

~ 🖥 ~

One company that offers genealogy data on CD-ROM is Everton Publishers. This company has been in the genealogy printing business for many years and is now offering some of their information on CD-ROM disc. One of their best known books is now available on CD-ROM: *The Handybook for Genealogists.* This disc contains scanned maps, a brief history of the settlement of each state, lists of genealogical libraries and societies, and lists of county courthouse addresses. This is a very useful reference for genealogists. Everton also offers collections of genealogy information that have been submitted to their bimonthly magazine, *Everton's Genealogical Helper.* These discs are called *Computerized Family File* and *Roots Cellar.* This collection contains approximately 100,000 family groupings from Everton's Family File 1 & 2, giving names, dates, places, and relationships for around 1,000,000 people, mostly in the U.S. and Europe, but there are also some entries for Latin America, Canada, the Pacific Islands, and Asia. *Root Cellar* contains names, dates, places, and the event being queried.

~ 🖥 ~

Another notable CD-ROM disc is produced by the New England Historic Genealogical Society, the oldest and largest genealogical society in North America. This society is well known for their publication of the *New England Historic and Genealogical Register*, the oldest continuously published genealogical journal in the world. This *Register* has been printed quarterly for 150 years. It not only treats definitively a sizable portion of New England's colonial and early nineteenth-century population, but it also provides one of the largest databases of names, facts, and printed primary sources available to anyone studying the first eight or so generations of American life. The Society has released a CD-ROM disc containing the New England Historic and Genealogical Register. This disc is a bit different than most others in that the journals were not OCR-scanned.

Instead, actual pictures of each page are on the CD-ROM disc and then an index of all names is available. The index links each name to the page(s) on which it appears. You then see an actual picture of the original journal page on your screen.

~▢~

Several other companies produce still more CD-ROM discs that may have some value to genealogists. This includes telephone directories so that you can find others of the same elusive surname. Another resource that is useful to some people is the Social Security Death Records. These only list deaths in the 1960s or later. Several companies produce these discs.

U.S. History on CD-ROM is produced by Bureau Development, Inc. and has approximately 100 older history books and other documents plus newer public domain materials all on one CD-ROM disc. While there is very little genealogy information on this CD-ROM, it is an excellent source of information on the events all throughout U.S. history. This can be an excellent method of finding the events that shaped your ancestors' lives.

Finally, the CD-ROM disc that is included with this book contains many reference materials of interest to genealogists. You will find lists of most of the genealogy societies, libraries, and archives in the United States and Canada. Also, several forms that may be imported into your word processor and then printed out are included. See the introductory materials on the CD-ROM disc itself for details.

Operating Systems

All the genealogy CD-ROM discs available today are for PC clone systems, either for MS-DOS or Windows. There are no genealogy CD-ROM discs on the market today for Macintosh. However, Macintosh owners should not despair; use of "PC emulator" software such as SoftPC or SoftWindows allows the Macintosh owner to use these CD-ROMs in the same manner as a PC owner would use them.

Photo CD: A Picture Is Worth 27 Megabytes

In 1990, Eastman Kodak Company introduced the Photo CD and the photography world has adopted the technology quickly. A Photo CD looks like any other CD or CD-ROM with the exception that it is normally a gold color instead of having the usual silver or aluminum appearance. Either new or existing photographs can be stored as very high resolution pictures on a Photo CD. There are different standards and resolution levels available; the higher quality resolutions allow the storage of magazine-quality pictures. As many as 100 normal photographs can be stored on a Photo CD.

The Photo CD not only is revolutionizing photography, it has impact on many other areas, including genealogy. Most genealogists collect old photographs of family members and many are using computers to sort and organize their data. Until recently, these old photographs were normally kept in a closet or a dresser drawer. The Photo CD now allows these photographs to become a part of the genealogy database and to be fully integrated with the information on the person's life. You can now see information about a person, then with a couple of keystrokes or mouse clicks the picture is displayed on the computer screen. Not all genealogy programs support Photo CD yet but several do and many more will in the future.

When taking new photographs, it is easy to send the entire roll of undeveloped film to a photofinishing service that offers both prints and Photo CDs. You can get these pictures transferred to disc for prices as low as 75 cents per image. For converting old pictures to scanned images on Photo CD the photo processor must do more manual work so prices are higher, typically $3.00 or so per picture when a number of pictures are sent at once. If you want the photos sorted in a specific order you will probably pay extra.

Creating a Photo CD is not something that is easily done on a home PC. The Kodak Photo CD Writer can cost $50,000 or more and attaches to a high-powered computer. Sun Sparc Stations are popular for this applications, a Sparc Station is several times more powerful than the fastest Pentium PC. However, many CD-ROM drives now found in PCs and Macintoshes can read Photo CDs.

~⬜~

Unlike a CD-ROM computer disc or an audio CD, the Photo CDs can be written to several times. The older photos cannot be erased or rewritten, but new photos may be appended to existing ones already on the disk. The Photo CD consists of several layers: a transparent substrate, a dye layer, a gold reflective layer, and a protective layer. It is the gold reflective layer that is different from CD-ROM discs which are normally aluminum. This gold reflective layer does allow for multiple "sessions" in which more photographs are added onto an existing Photo CD.

You can create printed pictures from Photo CD discs, but the cost of a printer that produces high-quality photographs is too high for most hobbyists. Several color inkjet printers are available today for under $500 that will reproduce pictures, but the quality will not approach that of the original photograph. You can send the Photo CD to a professional photofinish service. However, prices are normally cheaper to reproduce the original picture than it is to reproduce the picture on Photo CD. Color slides can be made from Photo CD pictures less expensively.

If you want to view Photo CDs on your computer, make sure that you purchase a CD-ROM drive that says "Photo CD compatible" or it may say "CD-ROM XA." The XA stands for Extended Architecture and is the standard for Photo CDs. Most CD-ROM drives manufactured today do conform to XA standards but you should double-check before purchasing that "bargain drive." Almost all Photo CD software available is for Windows or Macintosh or OS/2, there is almost none available for MS-DOS. To run Photo CD software on a Windows PC you will need at least a 386SX with 4MB of RAM memory. However, such a system will be very slow. A 486 with at least 8MB of memory is recommended, and more memory is desirable. Also, the color graphics board within the computer and the monitor itself must be capable of displaying 24-bit color. This is normally referred to as "16.7 million colors."

~⬜~

The Photo CD holds up to 100 images that have been digitized. Each picture is stored on a Photo CD five times, each picture is stored in five different resolution levels. The lowest level is used for a "thumbnail" photo The cover of the "jewel box" that contains the Photo CD typically has one index page showing all the thumbnail photos for quick identification. Each of the thumbnail photos is less than one-inch square. The third level of resolution, called "base resolution," is equal to that shown on a television set, while the highest level of resolution is full photography quality. The two highest resolution pictures are stored with a great deal of file compression, decoding them can be a bit slow. The lower three resolutions use no compression at all.

Photo CD images can be displayed on a television set using a CD player created for that purpose. When Photo CDs were first introduced, Eastman Kodak advertised this capability heavily and suggested that all future photo albums would be viewed on television sets. Sales of these television-compatible Photo CD players has languished but Eastman Kodak got a pleasant surprise when the sales of Photo CD-compatible computer CD-ROM drives far exceeded expectations. The fast growth in computer power and computer graphics in the home has enabled software producers to create applications that do far more than simply viewing still pictures on a screen. By integrating Photo CD graphics within genealogy programs and a multitude of other computer applications, Photo CD sales are increasing every year.

Photo CD-Compatible Genealogy Software

Although the list of Photo CD-compatible genealogy software is short, it is growing every year. At the time of this writing, the following programs offered at least some support for Photo CD:

- ➡ Family Tree Maker for Windows by Banner Blue Software
- ➡ Visual Family, a Windows shareware program
- ➡ Cumberland Family Tree for Windows

Of course Photo CD pictures can be converted to any of the other graphics formats, stored on a hard drive and then used in any genealogy program that supports pictures. That negates many of the advantages of Photo CD, however.

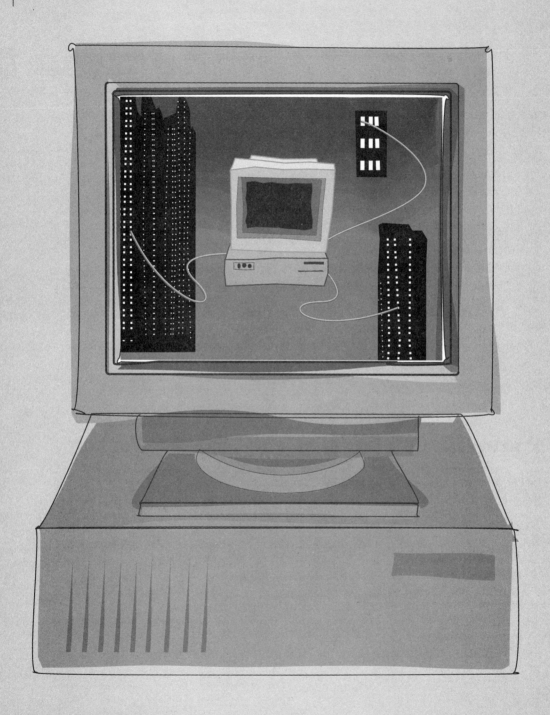

9 Connecting to the Mormon Databases

The

members of the Church of Jesus Christ of Latter-day Saints are often referred to as "the Mormons" and sometimes as "the LDS," which stands for "Latter-day Saints." This church is well known for their Family History Library in Salt Lake City and for their more than 1,100 local Family History Centers in North America and overseas. Teams of church members travel around the world making microfilm copies of public records that may be of interest to others who wish to research their ancestry.

Why does a church collect genealogy records? The church teaches its members that

- ➡ Every person's identity is eternal, life does not end at the time of death of the physical body.

- ➡ During a person's "earth life," he or she obtains a mortal body and joins a family. Family relationships can last into eternity.

- ➡ Each person must obtain baptism within the church. For those who died without being baptized or before such a baptism was available, a method has been provided so that they may be baptized posthumously. Such a baptism is considered voluntary; church members believe that the deceased person is able to accept or reject the baptism even though they now reside in the spirit world.

- ➡ Mormons conduct these baptisms and other religious ceremonies by proxy with a descendant standing in for the deceased ancestor. The religious requirement to identify each ancestor and to perform the religious ceremonies requires genealogy research.

The records collected by the Church of Jesus Christ of Latter-day Saints are available to church members and nonmembers alike in their huge Family History Library in Salt Lake City as well as at the Family History Centers throughout the world. Not only are these records available to nonchurch members, the LDS Church encourages nonmembers to use their facilities. At any given moment in the Family History Library or at local Family History Centers there are usually more nonmembers than LDS church members using the research facilities.

What Information Is Available?

The information available falls within seven classifications:

➡ About 1.5 million reels of microfilm are accessible, and most of them are copies of original records from around the world. Assuming that one reel of microfilm is equivalent to about 300 printed pages, this microfilm collection is the equivalent of about 450 million pages of information, making it the largest collection of genealogical information in the world. Almost all of these microfilms can be rented through a local Family History Center, there is no need to travel to Salt Lake City to view the microfilms.

➡ The Family History Library contains more than 165,000 genealogy books and reference books that do not normally go out on loan. However, where the authors have given permission or where copyrights have expired, some of these books have been microfilmed, and those microfilms may be rented in the local Family History Centers.

➡ International Genealogical Index (available on computer and on microfiche).

➡ Ancestral File (available on computer and on microfiche).

➡ Social Security Death Records (on computer only).

➡ Military Index (on computer only).

➡ Family History Library Catalog (on computer and on microfiche).

While the 1.5 million reels of microfilm and the books are important to every genealogist, we will focus on the computerized databases.

Network Access

One of the most common questions asked is "How do I access the Mormons' databases with my computer?" Unfortunately, you cannot connect directly by modem. There is no dial-up access or other online public access to the big databases in Salt Lake City.

However, there is free access to these databases provided by the LDS Church. It is not as convenient as modem access: You will need to visit a local Family History Center near you and use a computer equipped with a CD-ROM drive. The same databases that are in Salt Lake City are on the CD-ROM discs in the local Family History Center. Also, you may extract data from their databases and copy them to paper or to a floppy disk that you can take home with you. The data can be copied to disk either as ASCII text or as GEDCOM data. If copied in GED-COM format, that information may be imported directly into your favorite genealogy program without being retyped.

In Salt Lake City there is limited network access. The Family History Library's computer database became so popular that the church expanded the research facilities and placed additional computers in the Joseph Smith Memorial Building located a short distance from the Library. All of these computers are connected by Local Area Networks to an online version of their databases that emulates the CD-ROMs. While the Family History Library wishes to make this data available to people worldwide, they are proceeding cautiously with online access. Technical issues, support issues, and concerns about copyrights need to be resolved first, but online access to the LDS databases probably will be announced within a few years.

Local Family History Centers

Each of the Church's Family History Centers is owned and operated by a local LDS church. Many of them are located within church buildings, although a few may exist in local libraries or other facilities. The Family History Center near me is located in a small "strip mall" between a bank and an insurance agency. Each of these local Centers functions as a "catalog order office" for the large Library in Salt Lake City.

You can find listings of all the local Family History Centers online on CompuServe's Genealogy Forum in the "Salt Lake City records" library. These listings contain street addresses and usually the telephone numbers. It's a good idea to call before visiting in order to inquire about the hours they are open. The Family History Centers are operated by volunteers: the smaller ones may only be open three or four hours a week. Larger centers in major metropolitan areas may be open 60 hours a week or more.

If you do not have online access to these listings, you may find a local Mormon church listed in your telephone directory. Not every church contains a Family History Center, but the officials of each church will always know where the closest Center is. You may have to call several times before someone answers the telephone, as the smaller churches are not staffed all the time.

When you enter a local Family History Center, you will find microfilm and microfiche viewers and at least one computer that is equipped with a CD-ROM drive. Larger centers may have multiple computers. Computerized genealogy study is becoming very popular and there usually are not enough computer systems to meet the demand. Most local Centers have a reservation system where you sign up for computer time several days or weeks in advance. While restrictive, this method does assure that everyone has equal opportunity to use the CD-ROM discs. Again, there is no charge for using the computers. You may have to pay a modest fee for the paper you print on or for a floppy disk that you purchase.

When you visit your local Family History Center you can look at their catalogs of the millions of microfilms and microfiche available in Salt Lake City. These catalogs are available on both CD-ROM discs and microfiche. Once you have identified the microfilm that you want to view, you fill out a small order form for each roll. The order is sent by computer to Salt Lake City, and three to six weeks later you receive a postcard saying that your microfilms have been received. You then return to the local Family History Center to view the microfilms using their microfilm viewers; you cannot remove this microfilm from the Center. Most local Family History Centers have microfilm-to-paper copiers, you can make paper copies of the records that interest you and take those copies home.

The charge of approximately $3.00 is for a short rental of the microfilm. For a modest extra charge the film may be kept in the local Center for six months, allowing you plenty of time to search the entire reel. Also, some of the more popular microfilms may be available on permanent loan.

Who May Use the Family History Library's Information

The facilities of the Family History Library in Salt Lake City and the local Family History Centers are open to everyone regardless of religious affiliation. In fact, more non-LDS people use these records than do LDS members. Almost all the information recorded on microfilm or in the computers is available to the general public.

During my visits to both local Family History Centers and to the large Family History Library in Salt Lake City, no one has ever asked what my religion is. The local center near me does have a sign-in list for people who use their facility; when signing in one question asked is "Are you an LDS Member? (Yes/No)." That's the only question I have ever seen about a person's religion. Also, nobody at an LDS facility has ever discussed religion with me unless I first asked a question specifically about the LDS religion.

The officials of the Family History Library are very open with their data and they know that making their records open to everyone is the best method of ensuring that new data will be made available. Therefore, everyone is always welcome in their centers.

Microfilms versus Computer Databases

The Church of Jesus Christ of Latter-day Saints originally made their information available to everyone on microfilm and microfiche. Those are still the most popular information distribution methods, but the introduction of CD-ROM-equipped computers has greatly simplified the method of finding the information that you seek. In order to protect the privacy of living individuals, the data available is only on deceased persons or for people who have given permission for their names to be distributed. Most of the information available is for people born at least 100 years ago.

~🖳~

The *International Genealogical Index* is probably the best place to start looking for information about an ancestor that you know little about. The International Genealogical Index (I.G.I.) is an index of names of deceased persons for whom LDS temple ordinances have been performed. It provides birth, christening, and marriage information and may also contain a few other references, such as being listed in a census, mentioned in another person's will, or being listed in a document as a relative of someone else. The I.G.I. rarely lists dates of death as that date is not significant for LDS religious purposes; the church teaches that life is eternal.

The I.G.I. is available on both microfiche and on CD-ROM discs with the CD-ROM version having the advantage of being able to search all North American genealogy records at once. The microfiche versions are divided up by state or province; searching for an individual's records on microfiche can be painstaking when you do not know the state or province. The I.G.I. is available for the United States and Canada as well as for almost all other countries in the world that use the European-style alphabet. The information for the Orient, Arab countries, India, and for other countries with differing alphabets have generally not been computerized because of the difficulty in converting that data into a searchable database using normal keyboard input.

The I.G.I. may be searched for individuals' records in three different ways: by birth records, by marriage records, or by parents' names. The search is first by geographic area and then by surname and given name, and you may select to search either by exact spelling or by similar-sounding spellings. For instance, if you specify SMITH, the computers will optionally also show all SMYTHE and SMITHE entries. The information found will then reference the call number on the microfilm where the original data is found.

Each item in the I.G.I. is a free-standing record; generations are not linked together other than by the parent-child connection. You cannot obtain information on a family showing many generations from I.G.I. data.

The use of the I.G.I. is similar to the use of any index: you find the person in the index, note the call number of the microfilm and then order that microfilm to obtain the needed information. The person listed in the I.G.I. may not even be the person you seek, it may be someone else of the same name who lived in the same area at that time. Also, numerous errors in the extracted I.G.I. data exist. Only by examining the original data on microfilm can you be sure that the information is correct.

Information within the I.G.I. may be printed on paper, sent to a disk as a text file, or sent to disk as a GEDCOM file. The GEDCOM files have the advantage of being imported directly into a genealogy program. In most cases, you will not want to directly import unverified data into your primary genealogy database; you first create a new database and import the GEDCOM data into that empty database. You can then use the power of your favorite genealogy program to examine the data. Once you are satisfied with the accuracy, you may copy part or all of the newly obtained data directly into your primary database.

The *Ancestral File* is another huge database collected by the LDS Church. It contains information on millions of names worldwide, with all data contributed by both LDS members and nonmembers. These individuals submitted GEDCOM files of their ancestors on disks, and this information was appended to the Ancestral File. Since the data references millions of individuals and was obtained from so many sources, it is impossible for the LDS Church to verify the data. All information is distributed on an "as is" basis. Many of the submitters were dedicated genealogists who verified each piece of information, while others were not as meticulous. In some cases information within the Ancestral File contains "family traditions" and other information that may be inaccurate. All data needs to be independently verified.

Again, data from the Ancestral File may be directly printed on paper, copied to a disk as a text file, or copied to disk as a GEDCOM file. If GEDCOM format is selected, this data can then be directly imported into an empty database in your favorite genealogy program in the same manner discussed earlier. A major advantage of the Ancestral File is that it does link together multiple generations where the information has been submitted. If you are fortunate enough to find a particular ancestor listed in the Ancestral File, you may find five or more generations of earlier ancestors listed as well. Once verified for accuracy, this data can be imported directly into your genealogy database.

~🖥~

The *U.S. Social Security Death Index* contains the names of 39 million deceased persons who had Social Security numbers and whose deaths were reported to the Social Security Administration. It only contains those records that have been computerized. The Social Security Administration has computerized most of their records starting with deaths in 1962, although you may occasionally find earlier deaths listed as well. This is still not all the deaths reported in the United States, however. Many people were not covered by the Social Security system, such as railroad workers, school teachers, public employees, or others with private retirement plans. Also, the deaths of many people who died prior to retirement were never reported to the Social Security Administration simply because there was no need to do so. Still, for anyone looking for information on ancestors who died after 1962 this can be a valuable source of clues. This is one of the few databases available for twentieth-century research. The information normally shows date of birth (when known), the state in which the Social Security number was issued, and the place of residence at the time of death. The information found within the Social Security Death Index may be printed out or transferred to disk.

~🖥~

The *Military Index* is a listing of individuals who died in the Korean or Vietnam conflicts. The records cover from 1950 through 1975. The Military Index contains the birth and death dates for the deceased person, the place of residence, the place of death, and the rank and service number of the person. For Vietnam casualties it also shows marital status, religious affiliation, and race. The information found within the Military Index may be printed on paper or transferred to disk.

~🖥~

The *Family History Library Catalog* is an easy-to-use electronic card catalog of the Family History Library in Salt Lake City. It shows both printed books as well as the many reels of microfilm. Almost all the microfilms listed within this catalog can be ordered through a local Family History Center. While there are several methods of searching this catalog, the two most popular ones are the *Surname Search* and the *Locality Search*.

The Surname Search is the method used to quickly find all books that concern a particular surname. This may include books that are available on microfilm. The Surname Search is an excellent method of finding any previous research that has been done on a surname of interest.

The Locality Search is the method used to quickly locate records available on microfilm that deal with a particular city, town, parish, county, province, and so forth.

All the microfilms available from the Family History Library are listed by title in the Family History Library Catalog, but the majority of these microfilms have not yet had every name contained on the films added to the LDS databases. For instance, a microfilm of the birth, marriage, and death records of Bangor, Maine, for the years 1819 to 1891 will be listed in the computerized catalog as "Bangor (Maine). City Clerk. Town and vital records 1819–1891." In this case the full set of records requires four reels of microfilm and each one can be ordered separately. However, the names that appear within each microfilm reel are not yet indexed and therefore are not on the computer CD-ROM discs. If you know that an ancestor lived in that area within the years listed, you can find the microfilms as listed in the CD-ROM's information.

How to Access the Databases

The LDS databases are searched by software called FamilySearch that was written by the Church's programming staff. This software was designed to be used by anyone with only a minimum of computer knowledge. Its use is intuitive, with menus and other prompts available on most every screen. Pressing the F1 key displays a context-sensitive Help screen at any point.

The first selection, "Using the Computer" is an orientation exercise for anyone not familiar with computers. It shows where the various keys are located on the keyboard and explains the concepts of searching a CD-ROM database. The next five selections (Ancestral File, International Genealogical Index, U.S. Social Security Death Index, Military Index, and Family History Library Catalog) are

This menu will appear when you start the FamilySearch program, prompting you to select the appropriate database.

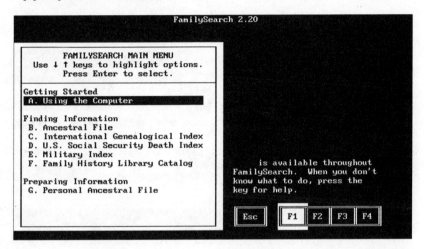

the CD-ROM databases available. The final selection, Personal Ancestral File, is a version of the LDS Church's popular MS-DOS genealogy program which is made available within Family History Centers for those who do not have access to a computer at home.

Selecting "International Genealogical Index" then loads the appropriate software to search that database. The user is first prompted for a country, with the U.S. and Canadian records being combined as "North America." Next, the user is prompted for the choice of "Individual Search, Marriage Search, or Parent Search." Use "Individual Search" and fill in the requested data. By pressing the F10 key you can filter by various selection criteria, such as the exact spelling of the surname, the location, the approximate year of marriage, or by a name combination.

It shows the marriage of Washington H. Eastman and Cynthia Tyler on 22 May 1831 in a civil record (a town clerk's record, not a church record) in Corinth, a small town in Penobscot County, Maine. Pressing Enter one more time shows that the original information can be found on microfilm M521631

This figure shows a marriage record from the International Genealogical Index for my great-great-grandparents.

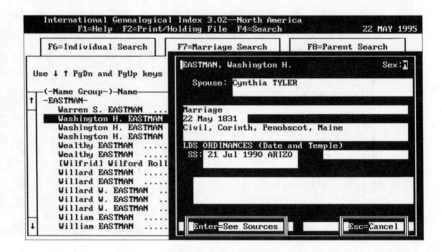

which includes the civil (town clerk's) records for Corinth, Penobscot County, Maine, for the years 1811 through 1895.

The I.G.I.'s birth records and parents' names records are searched in a fashion similar to the U.S. Social Security Death Index and the Military Index. The Ancestral File also uses similar commands but a few new details are introduced as the Ancestral File has the capability of linking together many generations.

Pressing Enter a couple of times displays details such as dates and places of birth, death, and burial. Whenever data is available, complete pedigrees may be displayed.

The CD-ROM databases available from the Church of Jesus Christ of Latter-day Saints are the most powerful computerized genealogy tools available today. Access to them is inexpensive although perhaps not as convenient as many people would like. Like all other secondary sources, the information obtained from the

This figure is an example of an Ancestral File search for John Fitzgerald Kennedy.

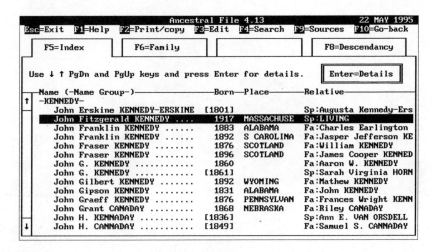

International Genealogical Index and the Ancestral File needs to be independently verified.

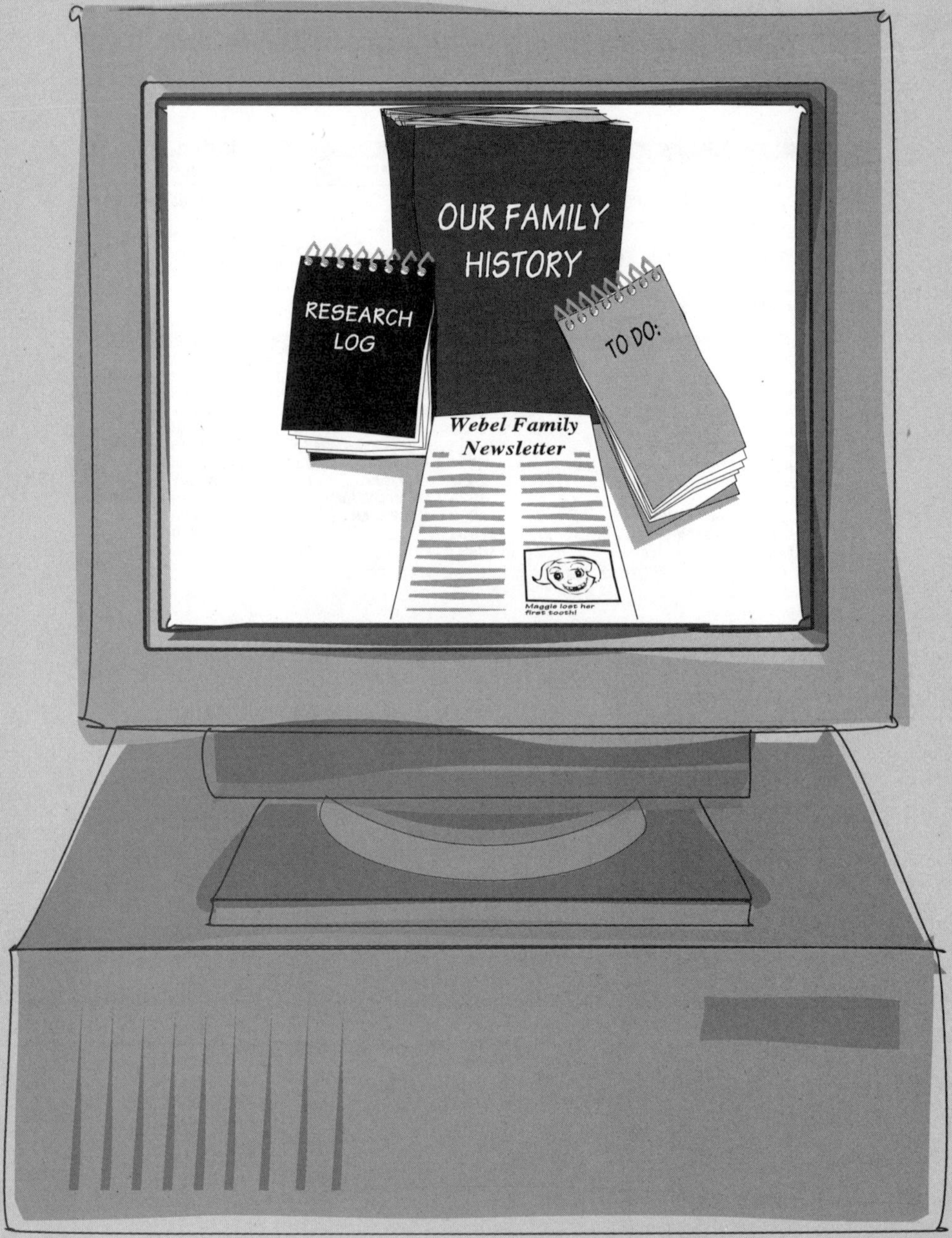
OUR FAMILY HISTORY
RESEARCH LOG
TO DO:
Webel Family Newsletter
Maggie lost her first tooth!

10

Now What? Where to Go from Here

Now

that you are about to finish reading this book, it's time to begin planning your search. You should create a "task list" or "research log" of things you wish to do. You can create this list on paper, but it's probably better to do so on a computer as you will be adding and deleting items on this list frequently. A properly organized to-do list will keep you focused and minimize any possibility of being sidetracked.

You will want to check available sources of data and find other genealogists working on the same families or in the same geographic areas. By doing so, you will speed up your own research efforts and you can probably help others in the process.

Once you have obtained a significant amount of genealogy data, you will probably want to share your information with others. Not only will your family members be interested in their ancestry, some of them may be able to add still more information that you were not able to obtain easily otherwise.

Creating the Initial Task List

Creating a task list can be done in many ways; a couple of genealogy programs will even do it for you. If you do have to generate such a list manually, it's probably best to keep it simple. I would suggest a list in four columns, with column #1 being the name of the individual, column #2 being the information you seek, column #3 being the location(s) that you wish to search for that data, and column #4 being a checkmark or the date in which that task was completed, as in the sample below:

Research Log

Name	Record Needed	Records/Location to Be Searched	Completed
Eastman, Washington Harvey	Census Records	National Archives, census records for 1830 through 1870	

Eastman, Washington Harvey	Will	Penobscot County Probate Court, Bangor, Maine records for 1887
Dubé, Louis	Christening record in 1676	"Répertoire Alphabétique des Mariages" by Drouin

Record Your Sources!

As always, record the source of every piece of information that you obtain. You will want to go back later and double-check your facts. It is not unusual to find a piece of information that contradicts something you obtained earlier; you will need to decide which is correct. One good method is to photocopy original documents wherever possible.

Always make sure that you write on the photocopy where the original was obtained. I still have a photocopy of a page from a genealogy book that gives critical information about the birthplace of one of my ancestors. I later found some information that was different and I suspected that the later data was erroneous. I pulled out the photocopied page from my filing cabinet and discovered to my horror that I never wrote down the name of the book nor even the name of the library where I photocopied the first page several years ago. I now have a photocopied page from an unknown book that is worthless in genealogy work. I have since learned always to photocopy the cover page when making copies of the pages of any book.

Obtain Genealogy Software

You will probably want to obtain some genealogy software to assist you in your work. There are several good ones described earlier in this book and new ones appear in the marketplace frequently. Whether you use Windows, MS-DOS, or a Macintosh, there are good genealogy programs available for you. Make sure that you obtain one that supports GEDCOM file imports and exports so that you may later transfer your data to a different program if you wish to.

Publishing Your Work

Once you have recorded much of your family's history, it will be time to share that information with other members of your immediate and extended family. Planning now will simplify the process of putting all the information together. Some genealogy programs will even generate a "genealogy book" for you, complete with pictures and charts.

Most genealogy books focus on one person and his or her descendants. This person frequently is the original immigrant to this country, although that won't be true in every instance. The book will then trace one line of descendants or, in the case of more ambitious genealogy studies, all of the known descendants of that ancestor. Most books are printed following the format of the *Register Plan* or the *Modified Register Plan,* in which every new generation is a new chapter in the book and a rigid numbering system is applied to every person mentioned. The genealogy programs that automatically generate genealogy books will normally use these formats.

For instance, the following is a chapter from a Register Plan printout of one family:

1   Washington Harvey[1] Eastman[1]. Born, 3 Apr 1810, in possibly Portland, Maine. Died, 22 May 1887, in Corinth, Penobscot Co., Maine. Burial in Evergreen Cemetery, Corinth, Penobscot Co., Maine. Occupation: Farmer.

Washington H. Eastman's birthplace is not yet known, but a town census in the 1830's and the Federal Census of 1840...... (Several pages of biographical details about this person follow but are deleted here for the sake of brevity.)

He married, first, Cynthia Tyler, daughter of Susan Marston, 22 May 1831. Born, 31 Jul 1797, in Bangor?, Penobscot Co., Maine. Died, 2 Dec 1845. Burial in Evergreen Cemetery, Corinth, Penobscot Co., Maine. Cynthia's maiden name is not yet proven. There's excellent circumstantial evidence that her maiden name was TYLER.
Children:

2   i. Elizabeth[2] Eastman.
     ii. Maria Eastman. Born, 26 Jul 1835.

3   iii. Orman Eastman.

He married, second, Sarah Nichols, daughter of Thomas Nichols and Elizabeth Hadlock, 28 Jan 1862, in Corinth, Penobscot Co., Maine. Born, Apr 1811. Died, 12 Dec 1888, in Penobscot Co., Maine. Burial in Evergreen Cemetery, Corinth, Penobscot Co., Maine.

Always tell the history simply and in a straightforward manner. Don't embellish it with flowery language or imaginative tales. Not every ancestor was a pillar of the community or a hero. Like a detective, a family historian records just the facts. Family stories certainly can certainly add color, however. Always include references as to where these stories were obtained. (You will probably want to use a little humor wherever appropriate.)

While you will want to include pictures of people and copies of documents within the book, limit the number and keep them simple. Generally speaking, the older the photograph or painting, the better. People will be interested in the wedding picture of their great-grandparents, but not everyone will appreciate a reproduction of your high school graduation picture. Maps, copies of old deeds, and other heirloom documents can also be very interesting to include in your book.

You should obtain as much information as possible about the earliest-known ancestor(s) listed in your book, then supplement that with as much information as possible about each descendent. As you come forward in time to the twentieth century you may prefer to be a bit more brief about the individuals listed. Again, the older records will generally be more interesting to most readers.

As for the unpleasant details of the story, finding the "black sheep" in the family tree in the 1700s can be very interesting, but similar information in the 1900s may not be as well received. As you come into the twentieth century, you will find that discretion is best in describing the personal weaknesses and tragedies of recent years. Not everyone appreciates reading about the drinking problems or the extramarital affairs of their parents or grandparents or other near relatives. While a genealogist will always record all facts, the question of which facts are to be shared with everyone else is a different issue. In short, consider your audience. Any piece of information that is unpleasant to living individuals is a candidate to be omitted from your book.

You may want to custom print a genealogy book as a holiday gift or as a present to a newborn child. Such books can be created one at a time and placed in three-ring binders or other inexpensive binders. However, many people have hundreds or possibly even a thousand copies professionally printed and bound by one of the "vanity presses." This can be an expensive undertaking and you will want to wait until your research efforts on that particular family line are completed or nearly completed before printing such a volume.

Seeing your own work in print is a particularly satisfying experience. It is even more satisfying when the volume is attractively bound and the information within it is presented in accordance with all the standard rules of genealogy research.

Organizing a Family Association and Publishing a Family Newsletter

You may wish to join or start a family association. This isn't just for your immediate relatives; it normally includes all the people descended from one particular ancestor or all the people interested in a particular surname. If the family name is less common, such as Eastman, the family association will probably be open to all people with that name in their family tree. For the more common surnames—such as Smith or Green or Johnson, or some of the others that are not quite that common—it is best to form an association for the descendants of a particular person of that name. For instance, "the descendants of Henry Smith of Charlestown, Massachusetts in 1637."

A major advantage of a family association is that it allows people with common interests to work together on establishing family trees for the entire group. Most family associations collect family group sheets from all their members and combine them into large family trees. A quarterly newsletter is a common means of communicating with members and of distributing the information gathered.

Finding people with the same surname and mailing invitations is easy with today's technology. Obtain a listing of all the people with that surname listed in the online telephone directory or on one of the CD-ROMs with the same information. The list is copied to disk, and you can then create a form letter and do a mail merge with the list of addresses. It is now possible to generate hundreds of such letters and envelopes in one evening.

In the beginning you may become the president, secretary, treasurer, correspondence secretary, and newsletter publisher of the association all rolled into one. But within a few months you will be able to recruit enough new members so that the work can be shared as necessary. Your objective should be to launch the idea and to gain enough momentum for others to notice and join the association. Then you can focus on the individual tasks that you enjoy the most, be it organizing or perhaps printing the newsletter.

Such newsletters should include family stories, any newly discovered records, and of course, announcements of reunions. Planning a large family reunion can also be an excellent activity by itself.

Sharing Your Work

Probably one of the most rewarding genealogy activities is making your research available to others. In past years this was possible only by printing genealogy books, which is an expensive method of sharing data if you wish to print enough copies to ensure that every genealogy library has a copy. A faster and much cheaper method of sharing data is now available in the computer age: You can make your GEDCOM files available to others.

There are several ways of doing this. While it is possible to exchange floppy disks with others via mail, this method is still slow and tedious and can be expensive if you are going to share with many other people. Also, there is no method of ensuring the availability of your data after your death. Uploading your data files to an online service such as CompuServe allows the data to be available to thousands of individuals at almost no cost to you. Finally, contributing to the Ancestral File that is maintained by the Mormons allows your information to be included with similar information obtained from thousands of other genealogists and made available on CD-ROMs. Again, this is at no cost to you other than the required postage, a disk or two, and an envelope.

The Ancestral File, described earlier in this book, links individuals into families and pedigrees, showing their ancestors and descendants. The file contains genealogical information about millions of people from throughout the world. This information includes names of individuals; their family relationships and pedigrees; and dates and places of birth, marriage, and death. The Ancestral File is one of the databases offered on CD-ROM at local Family History Centers around the world.

To prepare your information for the Ancestral File you must use a genealogy program that supports Ancestral File submissions in GEDCOM format. Many modern genealogy programs can do that; you need to check to see if your genealogy program is on the list of certified programs that have been tested for Ancestral File submissions. Next, you should search the latest version of the Ancestral File at a nearby Family History Center to see if someone has already contributed information about your ancestry. You don't want to duplicate data that is already in the Ancestral File.

You may contribute information about living persons but that data will not be displayed in the Ancestral File. In order to protect the privacy rights of living persons, the Ancestral File displays genealogical information for deceased persons only. If you contribute information for a person who lived within the last 95 years and for whom you have no date of death, the file usually displays only the word LIVING in place of the name or other information. When contributing information you should include as many generations as possible. Start with yourself or with your children. Include all children of your direct ancestors whenever possible.

When you are ready to contribute your data, you will need to have your genealogy program convert your data to a GEDCOM file. Be sure to record your name, address, and telephone number in your GEDCOM file. Your name and address will appear in Ancestral File as the contributor of this information. This enables others who use the file to coordinate research with you. They are instructed that this information is to be used for this purpose only. By providing your name and address, you consent to their inclusion in the file. Contributions without a name and address will not be accepted.

The GEDCOM file is then written to disk. There is no method of submitting Ancestral File contributions online; you can only mail a disk to the Family

History Library. If the file is large, your genealogy program should be able to spread the file over two or more disks. Write the following on the label of each disk:

- Ancestral File Submission
- Your name, address, and telephone number
- The genealogical program you are using
- Your computer's operating system (MS-DOS 6.2, for example)
- If a GEDCOM file fills more than one disk, label each disk with the name and telephone number of the contact person.

Mail your disks to:

> Family History Department
> ATTN: Ancestral File Contributions
> 50 East North Temple Street
> Salt Lake City, UT 84150

If you have any questions about contributing information to Ancestral File, call the FamilySearch Support Unit at 1-800-346-6044.

Appendix: Guide to the CD-ROM

The CD-ROM accompanying this book comes with an installation program that will copy the files and programs to your hard disk. If you prefer, you may copy the files directly to your hard disk by using the Windows File Manager.

The CD-ROM includes a copy of CompuServe Information Manager for Windows, also known as WinCIM. This program will connect you with CompuServe Information Service, the largest online service in North America. As a new member of CompuServe, you will be given several hours of free online time. During this time you can use the two genealogy services on CompuServe along with the more than 2,000 other services available. You will also have full access to the Internet with three hours of free online time per month above and beyond the free time on CompuServe.

You'll also find genealogy shareware and demo versions of commercial genealogy programs for Windows and for MS-DOS on the CD-ROM, as well as a database of almost 5,000 genealogy societies, libraries, and other archives that contain significant genealogy information. Other files on the CD-ROM contain numerous helpful text files about a variety of genealogy topics and genealogy forms that you can print out with your own word processor. The following is a summary of the CD-ROM contents:

What's on the CD-ROM

 Demos

Reunion for Windows from Leister Productions

Family Tree Maker for Windows from Banner Blue Software

Family Origins for Windows from Parsons Technology

The Master Genealogist, a powerful MS-DOS genealogy program from Wholly Genes Software

Roots IV, a popular MS-DOS genealogy program from CommSoft

Family Origins for MS-DOS from Parsons Technology

➔ Shareware
  Family Tree for Windows, a shareware Windows genealogy program
  Brothers Keeper, the most popular MS-DOS genealogy program

➔ Resources
  Dictionary of genealogy terms
  National Archives Regional Libraries addresses in order to help you find the nearest location of one of the major sources of genealogy information
  Vital Records Offices addresses throughout the United States
  Inquiry letters that you can customize with your word processor and then mail to others with the same surname
  Genealogy forms that you can print on your own printer with Microsoft Word, WordPerfect, or most other word processors
  Census Records Factfinder
  Information about the **National Genealogical Society**
  Information about the **New England Historic Genealogical Society**

➔ Database   A database containing the addresses of almost 5,000 genealogy societies, libraries and archives throughout the United States and Canada

➔ Online service   Free communications software that includes
  Free time on Ziffnet and the CompuServe Information Service
  Three hours of free time on the Internet

➔ Ziff-Davis Press   Information about many of Ziff-Davis Press's other computer books

System Requirements

386DX-33 (486DX-33 or faster recommended)
4MB RAM (minimum)
4MB available of hard drive
SuperVGA adapter (supporting 640 x 480 resolution and 256 colors) highly recommended

Microsoft mouse or 100 percent compatible

Microsoft Windows 3.1 or higher

MS-DOS 3.0 or higher

A CD-ROM drive (double-speed highly recommended)

In addition, the program interface makes use of the following standard Windows utilities:

WRITE.EXE

NOTEPAD.EXE

WINHELP.EXE

Preferences   By striking the F10 key, whenever the program is not busy, a preference dialog will appear. You may enable or disable the background music and transition effects.

Installing the CD-ROM

The installation will copy only a few files to your hard drive and then will create a program group and icons within the Windows Program Manager. Once installed, you may copy other files to your hard disk if you wish. To install the CD-ROM onto your hard drive,

1. Insert the CD-ROM into your CD-ROM drive.

2. From the File menu in the Windows Program Manager, select Run.

3. Enter the drive letter for your CD-ROM drive, followed by the command INSTALL. For instance, if your CD-ROM disk is configured as drive F, you would type: F:INSTALL

4. The Ziff-Davis Installation window appears. When prompted, click on the PROCEED button. Follow the instructions displayed to complete the installation.

Uninstalling the CD-ROM Icons

The installation process for this CD-ROM simply creates a "ZD Press" program group and program icons. To remove all trace of the CD-ROM from your system, just delete the "ZD Press" program group using the Program Manager's File/Delete menu items. Make sure the "ZD Press" group is selected before doing this.

If you made a change using the "Preferences" dialog box, a small file was created in your Windows directory, usually C:\WINDOWS, named ZDPROOTS.INI. You may delete this file.

Index

A

B

C

Ziff-Davis Press Survey of Readers

Please help us in our effort to produce the best books on personal computing.
For your assistance, we would be pleased to send you a FREE catalog
featuring the complete line of Ziff-Davis Press books.

1. How did you first learn about this book?

Recommended by a friend . . . . ☐ -1 (5)
Recommended by store personnel . . . . ☐ -2
Saw in Ziff-Davis Press catalog . . . . ☐ -3
Received advertisement in the mail . . . . ☐ -4
Saw the book on bookshelf at store . . . . ☐ -5
Read book review in: _____ ☐ -6
Saw an advertisement in: _____ ☐ -7
Other (Please specify): _____ ☐ -8

2. Which THREE of the following factors most influenced your decision to purchase this book? (Please check up to THREE.)

Front or back cover information on book . . . ☐ -1 (6)
Logo of magazine affiliated with book . . . . . . ☐ -2
Special approach to the content . . . . ☐ -3
Completeness of content . . . . ☐ -4
Author's reputation. ☐ -5
Publisher's reputation . . . . ☐ -6
Book cover design or layout . . . . ☐ -7
Index or table of contents of book . . . . ☐ -8
Price of book . . . . ☐ -9
Special effects, graphics, illustrations . . . . ☐ -0
Other (Please specify): _____ ☐ -x

3. How many computer books have you purchased in the last six months? _____ (7-10)

4. On a scale of 1 to 5, where 5 is excellent, 4 is above average, 3 is average, 2 is below average, and 1 is poor, please rate each of the following aspects of this book below. (Please circle your answer.)

Depth/completeness of coverage	5 4 3 2 1	(11)
Organization of material	5 4 3 2 1	(12)
Ease of finding topic	5 4 3 2 1	(13)
Special features/time saving tips	5 4 3 2 1	(14)
Appropriate level of writing	5 4 3 2 1	(15)
Usefulness of table of contents	5 4 3 2 1	(16)
Usefulness of index	5 4 3 2 1	(17)
Usefulness of accompanying disk	5 4 3 2 1	(18)
Usefulness of illustrations/graphics	5 4 3 2 1	(19)
Cover design and attractiveness	5 4 3 2 1	(20)
Overall design and layout of book	5 4 3 2 1	(21)
Overall satisfaction with book	5 4 3 2 1	(22)

5. Which of the following computer publications do you read regularly; that is, 3 out of 4 issues?

Byte . . . . ☐ -1 (23)
Computer Shopper . . . . ☐ -2
Home Office Computing . . . . ☐ -3
Dr. Dobb's Journal . . . . ☐ -4
LAN Magazine . . . . ☐ -5
MacWEEK . . . . ☐ -6
MacUser . . . . ☐ -7
PC Computing . . . . ☐ -8
PC Magazine . . . . ☐ -9
PC WEEK . . . . ☐ -0
Windows Sources . . . . ☐ -x
Other (Please specify): _____ ☐ -y

Please turn page.

6. What is your level of experience with personal computers? With the subject of this book?

	With PCs	With subject of book
Beginner.	☐ -1 (24)	☐ -1 (25)
Intermediate.	☐ -2	☐ -2
Advanced.	☐ -3	☐ -3

7. Which of the following best describes your job title?

Officer (CEO/President/VP/owner). . . . . ☐ -1 (26)
Director/head. . . . . ☐ -2
Manager/supervisor. ☐ -3
Administration/staff. . . . . ☐ -4
Teacher/educator/trainer. . . . . ☐ -5
Lawyer/doctor/medical professional. . . . . . . ☐ -6
Engineer/technician. ☐ -7
Consultant. . . . . ☐ -8
Not employed/student/retired. . . . . ☐ -9
Other (Please specify): _____ ☐ -0

8. What is your age?

Under 20. . . . . ☐ -1 (27)
21-29. . . . . ☐ -2
30-39. . . . . ☐ -3
40-49. . . . . ☐ -4
50-59. . . . . ☐ -5
60 or over. . . . . ☐ -6

9. Are you:

Male. . . . . ☐ -1 (28)
Female. . . . . ☐ -2

Thank you for your assistance with this important information! Please write your address below to receive our free catalog.

Name: _____

Address: _____

City/State/Zip: _____

Fold here to mail.

3261-16-20

■ END-USER LICENSE AGREEMENT

READ THIS AGREEMENT CAREFULLY BEFORE BUYING THIS BOOK. BY BUYING THE BOOK AND USING THE PROGRAM LISTINGS, CD-ROM, AND PROGRAMS REFERRED TO BELOW, YOU ACCEPT THE TERMS OF THIS AGREEMENT.

The program listings included in this book and the programs included on the CD-ROM contained in the package on the opposite page ("CD-ROM") are proprietary products of Ziff-Davis Press and/or third party suppliers ("Suppliers"). The program listings and programs are hereinafter collectively referred to as the "Programs." Ziff-Davis Press and the Suppliers retain ownership of the CD-ROM and copyright to the Programs, as their respective interests may appear. The Programs and the copy of the CD-ROM provided are licensed (not sold) to you under the conditions set forth herein.

License. You may use the CD-ROM on any compatible computer, provided that the CD-ROM is used on only one computer and by one user at a time.

Restrictions. You may not commercially distribute the CD-ROM or the Programs or otherwise reproduce, publish, or distribute or otherwise use the CD-ROM or the Programs in any manner that may infringe any copyright or other proprietary right of Ziff-Davis Press, the Suppliers, or any other party or assign, sublicense, or otherwise transfer the CD-ROM or this agreement to any other party unless such party agrees to accept the terms and conditions of this agreement. This license and your right to use the CD-ROM and the Programs automatically terminates if you fail to comply with any provision of this agreement.

U.S. GOVERNMENT RESTRICTED RIGHTS. The CD-ROM and the programs are provided with **RESTRICTED RIGHTS**. Use, duplication, or disclosure by the Government is subject to restrictions as set forth in subparagraph (c)(1)(ii) of the Rights in Technical Data and Computer Software Clause at DFARS (48 CFR 252.277-7013). The Proprietor of the compilation of the Programs and the CD-ROM is Ziff-Davis Press, 5903 Christie Avenue, Emeryville, CA 94608.

Limited Warranty. Ziff-Davis Press warrants the physical CD-ROM to be free of defects in materials and workmanship under normal use for a period of 30 days from the purchase date. If Ziff-Davis Press receives written notification within the warranty period of defects in materials or workmanship in the physical CD-ROM, and such notification is determined by Ziff-Davis Press to be correct, Ziff-Davis Press will, at its option, replace the defective CD-ROM or refund a prorata portion of the purchase price of the book. **THESE ARE YOUR SOLE REMEDIES FOR ANY BREACH OF WARRANTY.**

EXCEPT AS SPECIFICALLY PROVIDED ABOVE, THE CD-ROM AND THE PROGRAMS ARE PROVIDED "AS IS" WITHOUT ANY WARRANTY OF ANY KIND. NEITHER ZIFF-DAVIS PRESS NOR THE SUPPLIERS MAKE ANY WARRANTY OF ANY KIND AS TO THE ACCURACY OR COMPLETENESS OF THE CD-ROM OR THE PROGRAMS OR THE RESULTS TO BE OBTAINED FROM USING THE CD-ROM OR THE PROGRAMS AND NEITHER ZIFF-DAVIS PRESS NOR THE SUPPLIERS SHALL BE RESPONSIBLE FOR ANY CLAIMS ATTRIBUTABLE TO ERRORS, OMISSIONS, OR OTHER INACCURACIES IN THE CD-ROM OR THE PROGRAMS. THE ENTIRE RISK AS TO THE RESULTS AND PERFORMANCE OF THE CD-ROM AND THE PROGRAMS IS ASSUMED BY THE USER. FURTHER, NEITHER ZIFF-DAVIS PRESS NOR THE SUPPLIERS MAKE ANY REPRESENTATIONS OR WARRANTIES, EITHER EXPRESS OR IMPLIED, WITH RESPECT TO THE CD-ROM OR THE PROGRAMS, INCLUDING BUT NOT LIMITED TO, THE QUALITY, PERFORMANCE, MERCHANTABILITY, OR FITNESS FOR A PARTICULAR PURPOSE OF THE CD-ROM OR THE PROGRAMS. IN NO EVENT SHALL ZIFF-DAVIS PRESS OR THE SUPPLIERS BE LIABLE FOR DIRECT, INDIRECT, SPECIAL, INCIDENTAL, OR CONSEQUENTIAL DAMAGES ARISING OUT THE USE OF OR INABILITY TO USE THE CD-ROM OR THE PROGRAMS OR FOR ANY LOSS OR DAMAGE OF ANY NATURE CAUSED TO ANY PERSON OR PROPERTY AS A RESULT OF THE USE OF THE CD-ROM OR THE PROGRAMS, EVEN IF ZIFF-DAVIS PRESS OR THE SUPPLIERS HAVE BEEN SPECIFICALLY ADVISED OF THE POSSIBILITY OF SUCH DAMAGES. NEITHER ZIFF-DAVIS PRESS NOR THE SUPPLIERS ARE RESPONSIBLE FOR ANY COSTS INCLUDING, BUT NOT LIMITED TO, THOSE INCURRED AS A RESULT OF LOST PROFITS OR REVENUE, LOSS OF USE OF THE CD-ROM OR THE PROGRAMS, LOSS OF DATA, THE COSTS OF RECOVERING SOFTWARE OR DATA, OR THIRD-PARTY CLAIMS. IN NO EVENT WILL ZIFF-DAVIS PRESS' OR THE SUPPLIERS' LIABILITY FOR ANY DAMAGES TO YOU OR ANY OTHER PARTY EVER EXCEED THE PRICE OF THIS BOOK. NO SALES PERSON OR OTHER REPRESENTATIVE OF ANY PARTY INVOLVED IN THE DISTRIBUTION OF THE CD-ROM IS AUTHORIZED TO MAKE ANY MODIFICATIONS OR ADDITIONS TO THIS LIMITED WARRANTY.